Twelve Ways to
Save Democracy in Wisconsin

Twelve Ways to
Save Democracy in Wisconsin

Matthew Rothschild

THE UNIVERSITY OF WISCONSIN PRESS

Publication of this book has been made possible, in part, through support
from the Anonymous Fund of the College of Letters and Science
at the University of Wisconsin–Madison.

The University of Wisconsin Press
728 State Street, Suite 443
Madison, Wisconsin 53706
uwpress.wisc.edu

Gray's Inn House, 127 Clerkenwell Road
London EC1R 5DB, United Kingdom
eurospanbookstore.com

Printed in the United States of America
This book may be available in a digital edition.

Library of Congress Cataloging-in-Publication Data

Names: Rothschild, Matthew, author.
Title: Twelve ways to save democracy in Wisconsin / Matthew Rothschild.
Description: Madison, Wisconsin : The University of Wisconsin Press, [2021]
Identifiers: LCCN 2021008779 | ISBN 9780299334949 (paperback)
Subjects: LCSH: Democracy—Wisconsin. | Wisconsin—
Politics and government—1951-
Classification: LCC JK6016 .R68 2021 | DDC 320.9775—dc23
LC record available at https://lccn.loc.gov/2021008779

To
JEAN,
the one and only

The cure for the ills of democracy is more democracy.

—Fighting Bob La Follette

Contents

Acknowledgments

First, I'd like to thank the staff at the Wisconsin Democracy Campaign for educating me on many of these issues over the past six years. I had only a passing knowledge of campaign finance laws and of gerrymandering when I arrived, and they showed a lot of patience while they schooled me. I'm grateful for the expertise that Michael Buelow, David Julseth, and Beverly Speer shared and for reading this manuscript and offering their advice. I appreciate the work on the business side of the Wisconsin Democracy Campaign from Evan Arnold and Barb Kneer, who keep the lights on. And I'm thrilled that Cely Flores has joined our staff. I also want to give a shout-out to our longtime intern John Montgomery, who has provided invaluable research for our reports and stalwart assistance at our table at the Dane County Farmers' Market.

I want to thank the board of directors of the Wisconsin Democracy Campaign for their conscientious (yet uncompensated) stewardship: Peter Cannon, Erin Grunze, Bill Franks, Sue Lloyd, Beauregard Patterson, Mary Rouse, board chair Abby Swetz, Angie Trudell Vasquez, and Alfonso Zepeda-Capistrán. And I would like to thank our previous board chairs, Peter Skopec and Diane Welsh.

We at the Wisconsin Democracy Campaign are able to track and expose money in politics and advocate for a full democracy because of the donations from concerned citizens across this state, and I want to thank those individual donors, large and small, for supporting us and for putting up with my incessant begging. I'm especially grateful to Jeff Chandler, Pat and Dan Cornwell, George Cutlip, Susan Eichhorn, Beth Kubly, Tom Link, Dick Mazess, Al and Aileen Nettleton, Edward Ream, and Warren Werner not only for their generosity over the years but for their friendship as well.

I also want to thank the Brico Fund, the Brookby Foundation, the Buck Foundation, the Evjue Foundation, the Joyce Foundation, and the Craig Newmark Philanthropies for supporting the work of the Wisconsin Democracy Campaign.

I'm indebted to Gail Shea for having the vision to found the Wisconsin Democracy Campaign back in 1995, and to Mike McCabe, who ran it with gusto for fifteen years.

Then there's the impressive group of coalition partners we work with on a regular basis. One of the underreported stories in Wisconsin is how pro-democracy nonprofit leaders across the state are rowing harmoniously together, so let me salute the ones I interact with the most: Carlene Bechen of the Fair Elections Project, Anjali Bhasin of Wisconsin Conservation Voices, Julie Bomar of the Wisconsin Farmers Union, Heather DuBois Bourenane of the Wisconsin Public Education Network, Sachin Chheda of the Fair Elections Project, Debra Cronmiller of the League of Women Voters of Wisconsin, Sara Eskrich of Democracy Found, Kevin Gundlach of the South Central Federation of Labor, Jay Heck of Common Cause Wisconsin, Anita Johnson of Souls to the Polls, Greg Jones of the NAACP Dane County, Robert Kraig of Citizen Action, Angela Lang of Black Leaders Organizing for Communities, David Liners of WISDOM, Lisa Lucas of Wisconsin Voices, Rabbi Bonnie Margulis of Wisconsin Faith Voices for Justice, Helen Marks Dicks of AARP, Christine Neumann-Ortiz of Voces de la Frontera, Shauntay Nelson of All Voting Is Local, Chris Ott and Molly Collins of the ACLU of Wisconsin, George Penn of Wisconsin United to Amend, Kerry Schumann of Conservation Voters of Wisconsin, Ken Taylor of Kids Forward, Liz Trevino of All on the Line, and Markasa Tucker of the African American Roundtable. I enjoy working with all of you, and I'm amazed by all you do.

Democracy reform has some champions in the state legislature, so I tip my hat to: representatives Deb Andraca, Jimmy Anderson, David Bowen, Jonathan Brostoff, Dave Considine, Jodi Emerson, Dianne Hesselbein, Todd Novak, Sondy Pope, Melissa Sargent, Katrina Shankland, Mark Spreitzer, Shelia Stubbs, Lisa Subeck, Robyn Vining, Don Vruwink, and state senators Tim Carpenter, Rob Cowles, Jon Erpenbach, Gary Hebl, LaTonya Johnson, Chris Larson, Jeff Smith, and Lena Taylor. And I want to thank former state representatives Terese Berceau, Spencer Black, David Crowley, Andy Jorgensen, Penny Bernard Schaber, Chris Taylor, and JoCasta Zamarripa, along with former state senators Tim Cullen and Dave Hansen, former lieutenant governor Barbara Lawton, and former US senator Russ Feingold for all they've done over the years on this front.

I would like to give a special shout-out to former Republican state senator and majority leader Dale Schultz, whom I've come to know as a friend over the last five years. We call each other up and get together now and again at Ale Asylum to share tidbits and to bounce ideas around, which is the kind of exercise I like. I've got a quote of Dale's on my office wall: "When some think tank comes up with the legislation and tells you not to fool with it, why are you even a legislator anymore? . . . You're kind of a feudal serf for the folks with a lot of money."

I've been fortunate to do prodemocracy work for forty years now, and I couldn't have done it without my parents' guidance, the support of my brothers and sisters, and the sustenance of my high school friend Vic Schaffner, my friend from Nader days Carl Mayer, and all our friends who share in the commitment to make our world a more just place. Thanks to Joe Boucher, Marcie Brost and Dave Porterfield, Ron Binter and Janie Eggl, Debbie and Gilles Bousquet, Doug Bradley and Pam Shannon, Pat DiBiase and Allen Ruff, Charity Eleson and Steve Feren, Gail Gredler and Phil Schradle, Rick and Janet Gordon, Lynn Hobbie and Kevin Little, Glenda Hodge, Diane Hulick, Mike Kepler and Mary Beth Keppel, Mary and Ed Musholt, Bob McChesney and Inger Stole, Amit and Deepa Pal, Betsy Parker and Gerry Cumpiano, Ann and Joel Sacks, Jana and Don Sellarole, Kelly Parks Snider and John Snider, Gordy and Nancy Ranum, and Mary Reed.

Thanks also to the irreducible core of Madison activists, who turn this city into a "treehouse without a tree," to borrow an image from Adrienne Rich.

A word of advice to you, the reader: do your political work with friends. It's much easier—and more fun!—that way.

Sadly, I lost three of my friends while writing this book. George Shalabi was a warm and kind and proud advocate of progressive causes, especially Palestinian rights. Dan Wisniewski served many progressive elected leaders in our state, and he championed our environment in retirement—and tutored me on state politics. Mike Cassidy shared with me a love of language—and displayed an enviable playfulness. I salute all three.

Let me add another word, if I may, to all of you who hurtle yourselves into good causes: have hobbies outside of politics. I'm grateful to my friends on the tennis court, at the card table, and out birdwatching who've diverted me when I needed diversion.

This book would not have been possible without the wise guidance of Nathan MacBrien, editor at the University of Wisconsin Press, who steered me in the right direction while we were having coffee a couple of times at the Memorial Union. I'm also indebted to Sheila McMahon at UW Press for shepherding this manuscript through in such a professional manner. And I bow my head to the indefatigable Diana Cook, the best copyeditor and proofreader on the planet—or at least on planet Wisconsin. (She has been the proofreader for *The Progressive* magazine for about five decades now!)

I also appreciate the encouragement I got from UW political science professor Kathy Cramer, author of the crucial book *The Politics of Resentment* (2016), and the advice from UW journalism professor Lew Friedland, who is doing urgent work on the ailing media ecosystem in Wisconsin, and from Tim Slekar, the dean of the School of Education at Edgewood College.

I owe a debt of gratitude to the engaged writers who showed me the way, chief among them Wendell Berry, Edwidge Danticat, June Jordan, Terry Tempest Williams, and Howard Zinn.

I would like to thank our children—Katherine, Sam, and William—just for being who they are.

And most of all, I would like to thank my sweet wife, Jean, not only because this book was her idea in the first place but preeminently because she's a wonderful person, she's the love of my life, and she's the best partner anyone could ever ask for.

Twelve Ways to
Save Democracy in Wisconsin

Introduction

Wisconsin used to have a reputation as a laboratory of democracy. But that reputation has been badly tarnished in recent years. We've become more like a laboratory of oligarchy, with the corporate interests calling the shots.

We have a crisis of representation in Wisconsin.

Today, on many policy issues, what the people of Wisconsin want they don't get. Because of gerrymandering, because of the increasing role played by the superrich and corporations in our politics, because of voter suppression, and because of other trends that I'll be discussing, our elected officials often don't care what their constituents want. To an alarming degree, they view their donors as their constituents rather than the voters themselves.

As the executive director of the Wisconsin Democracy Campaign over the past six years, I've seen the dysfunction of our democracy up close and personal. But I've also seen some elected officials and a lot of nonprofit organizations and grassroots activists putting their shoulder to the wheel of our democracy and gaining some traction.

To honor their work and to provide a road map forward, I figured I would try to sketch out twelve ways to save our democracy.

The reforms that I'm offering are not the only twelve out there. In writing this book, I found it hard to boil down the list to just twelve, and I'm sure other political activists or scholars would come up with a somewhat different list.

Representative Katrina Shankland, whom I interviewed for this book and who has taken the lead on championing local control, insisted to me: "When it comes to democracy, the number one issue is making government more accessible." She said we need to have "democracy workshops" so more citizens can get involved. I acknowledge the need for more civic education, but it didn't make my final cut.

Beverly Speer, my colleague at the Wisconsin Democracy Campaign, strongly recommended that transparency be one of the top twelve issues. I'm a big advocate of transparency, and I discuss the need for transparency in the chapter on campaign finance, but I chose not to make it a stand-alone chapter.

My friend Patrick Barrett, managing director of the Havens Wright Center for Social Justice at the University of Wisconsin–Madison, stressed the importance of moving from single-member districts to multimember districts, as well as having proportional representation and modifying how the US Senate is constructed. And while I see merit in those ideas, I left these out.

Some other reforms—like ending the Electoral College or providing statehood to the District of Columbia—are crucial for our democracy nationally but not particularly germane to us here in Wisconsin.

One idea that is germane to Wisconsin is limiting the governor's veto power. The line-item veto, as it stands now, allows the governor to take a word out of a sentence to give it the opposite meaning from what the legislature intended (e.g., changing "shall not" to "shall"). That's absurd! But until we fix the problem of gerrymandering, the only person who truly represents a majority of Wisconsin voters is the governor, so it doesn't make sense to solve the line-item veto first because then a rigged and unrepresentative legislature could dominate even more than it does now.

One final idea that I don't address squarely in this book is how to combat the resurgent far-right forces of antidemocracy, which Donald Trump galvanized and which we saw materialize in all their violent ugliness at the US Capitol on January 6, 2021. These forces are a huge threat to our democracy, both here in Wisconsin and around the country. But tackling this topic would require another book in itself.

Here is a guide for you, the reader.

First, in each of the twelve chapters, I lay out the background on the issue, often in story form, and then I offer solutions to that particular problem. Next I have a section called Counterarguments and Complexities, where I respond to opposing points of view and grapple with some tricky implications. If you don't want to get in the weeds with me, you can skip to the next reform, but I hope you'll appreciate the discussions.

Second, the last two reforms that I propose—an all-out effort to uproot racism and a push toward economic democracy—cover such large topics and have such national dimensions that I created a separate part for them. And while it's true that some of the other reforms have a national scope and beg for a national solution—such as curbing money in politics, or outlawing gerrymandering, or reforming the media—these two issues of racism and economic inequality are so deep that I gave them special attention. Of course, the fundamental issue of racism shows up explicitly in some of the other chapters, such as the ones on gerrymandering, prison gerrymandering, and voter suppression. And if we had anything close to economic equality in this country, then the problem of money in politics wouldn't be nearly as enormous as it is now, since everyone could use their marbles in the political game if they wanted to. So listen for echoes and reverberations across chapters.

Third, I have an enlarged appendix. It's not a clinical condition but a way for me to offer you a couple of the speeches I've given over the last few years and a bit of advice for activists. I hope you'll enjoy reading these breezier offerings.

One last thing: I finished this manuscript on February 1, 2021. I'm sure there will be a lot of pertinent events in the ensuing months that cry out for inclusion here, but my typing hands are tired and I have no crystal ball.

I look forward to hearing what's on your Top Twelve list for prodemocracy reforms in Wisconsin. And I look forward to engaging in the public conversation and the political agitation to make our lists a reality—and to make Wisconsin once again a laboratory of democracy.

Part I

chapter 1

Ban Gerrymandering

Gerrymandering is an all-American term. It refers to the manipulative drawing of district maps to give an advantage to the political party in power, and the term dates back more than two hundred years. In 1812, Massachusetts governor Elbridge Gerry redrew a political district in a weird shape that looked like some mythic salamander, so people put "Gerry" together with "salamander" to get "gerrymander," and it's a term that's caught on ever since.

And it's a practice that's caught on. Both parties do it, and it's wrong whether Democrats are rigging the maps or Republicans are rigging the maps.

Redistricting is a constitutional obligation that every state has to fulfill every ten years after the census is done to make sure that each district has roughly equal numbers of people in it. The question is, Who does the redistricting? And how?

In 2009, the Democrats held all the levers of power in Wisconsin, with a Democratic governor and Democrats in control of the senate and the assembly. Good-government groups were pressuring them to enact independent, nonpartisan redistricting reform, akin to what Iowa had adopted three decades before. In Iowa, career civil servants draw the maps, and they are prohibited from using data on how precincts have voted in the past when drawing new maps. They are also required to draw compact and contiguous districts, and to respect local community and county boundaries to the fullest extent possible. Legislators then have to approve the maps in an up-or-down vote.

Democratic representative Spencer Black introduced a bill in 2009, as he had previously, to ban partisan gerrymandering and to adopt the Iowa model for redrawing the political maps.

After the 2000 census, Black was minority leader in the assembly, and he had seen, firsthand, how elected officials of both parties viewed redistricting simply as a tool to gain partisan advantage. He was so disgusted by this, and by the millions of taxpayer dollars spent on the legal wrangling over the maps, that he became a convert to the cause of fair maps.

"We should have independent redistricting," Black told me. "Basically, we do not have an election for control of the state legislature anymore" because gerrymandering has predetermined which candidates are going to win. "This deprives people of the right to choose who they want, and legislators don't fear accountability because they're not worried about losing their power."

Jeff Smith, then a Democratic representative who chaired the Elections and Campaign Reform Committee, favored Black's bill in 2009 and held a hearing on it.

"If you believe in what you're doing, you should be happy to have a level playing field," Smith told me, looking back. "I've been kicking myself for ten years now because I should have worked harder" for the bill's passage. (Smith is now a state senator.)

But some in the Democratic caucus were opposed to the bill. Political power is an intoxicating drug, and, thinking they were going to win again in 2010, they planned on rigging the maps their way when they did. One Democratic official even floated the idea of rigging the maps in their own favor, ahead of time, in 2009. "You know, the way the law is written, we could redistrict it right now," the official said.

But Smith would have none of that. "I just stood up and said, 'No, no way, we're not going to do that.'"

As you can see, some Democrats wanted to take the low road, and some wanted to take the high road.

Little did any of them know just how low a road the Republicans were about to take when, in the 2010 elections, Republicans got a clean sweep, taking over both chambers in the legislature and landing Scott Walker in the governor's chair.

Once the census was completed, the Republican leadership wasted no time in carrying out one of the worst gerrymanders in modern American history.

Redrawing the maps is the people's business, but they didn't do the people's business in the People's House. Instead, they went across the street from the capitol and holed up in the cushy law offices of Michael Best &

Friedrich, in a room that became known as the Map Room. It was a locked room. Two young staffers to the Speaker held the keys to the Map Room. The public wasn't allowed in. The media wasn't allowed in. Democrats weren't allowed in. Even Republican legislators who weren't in leadership weren't allowed into the locked Map Room unless they got permission from those young staffers. Once they were allowed in, these legislators were allowed to look at only their own redrawn districts. And before they could leave the locked Map Room, they had to sign an oath of secrecy.

That's not how the people's business should be carried out. In fact, that's 180 degrees from open and transparent government.

Inside the Map Room, the Republican leaders and their staff, along with a political scientist they hired from the University of Oklahoma, Keith Gaddie, set to work fixing the maps. Using data about the voting histories of individual precincts, they moved lines here or there on a map on their computers and were able to forecast how many more seats Republicans might gain. They didn't draw just one map. They offered the Republican leadership nine different incarnations of maps, each successive one predicting an even greater Republican majority, while keeping constant the number of people likely to vote Democratic and Republican. The only things that changed were the lines on the map.

They used two techniques to accomplish this deceitful goal. The first, called "packing," stuffed many Democratic areas into fewer and fewer districts, leaving the other districts more Republican. The other, called "cracking," split a Democratic-leaning city, like Sheboygan or Marshfield, and dragged half of its voters into a very rural and Republican area to the northwest, say, or dragged half of them into a very rural and Republican area to the southwest. By diluting the Democratic strongholds, they could turn an assembly district from blue to red.

The Republican leadership chose one of the most aggressive maps and then rammed it through the legislature in a matter of days. Governor Walker quickly signed the gerrymandered maps into law, and guess what? They worked great!

Just as they had predicted, Republicans were able to solidify their hold on power by virtue of these new maps.

With the old maps in 2010, Republicans had won about 250,000 more assembly votes than Democrats statewide, and they won sixty out of the ninety-nine seats in the assembly, as you might expect. Then in 2012, Democrats won about 170,000 more assembly votes than Republicans statewide—

a swing of about 420,000 votes for Democrats. But under the newly rigged maps, Republicans still won sixty out of the ninety-nine seats.

The gerrymandering was so blatant that a group of Democratic plaintiffs successfully sued in federal court in what became known as the *Whitford* case. In November 2016, a three-judge panel, in an opinion written by judge Kenneth Francis Ripple, an appointee of president Ronald Reagan, ruled that the gerrymandering violated the First Amendment and Fourteenth Amendment rights of the plaintiffs.

"It is clear that the drafters got what they intended to get," wrote Judge Ripple. "It secured for Republicans a lasting Assembly majority. It did so by allocating votes among the newly created districts in such a way that, in any likely electoral scenario, the number of Republican seats would not drop below 50 percent."

The three-judge panel then unanimously ordered the Republican leadership to go back and redraw the maps in a constitutional manner so that voters in Wisconsin would no longer be burdened with voting in districts whose boundaries were drawn in a hyperpartisan manner.

But that never happened. Attorney general Brad Schimel, defending his Republican colleagues, appealed to the US Supreme Court and asked for a stay of this decision, which was granted. The court heard the case in October 2017 and on June 18, 2018, remanded it back to the lower court, ruling that the plaintiffs didn't have sufficient "standing" because they hadn't proved individualized harm in their specific districts.

But justice Elena Kagan offered the plaintiffs a new line of argument: The rigged maps interfered with the plaintiffs' First Amendment right of association, and this interference does not have to be proven district by district. Every member of whichever party is being disadvantaged by the gerrymander suffers from the violation of this right, she wrote: "Members of the 'disfavored party' in the State, deprived of their natural political strength by a partisan gerrymander, may face difficulties fundraising, registering voters, attracting volunteers, generating support from independents, and recruiting candidates to run for office (not to mention eventually accomplishing their policy objectives)."

The lawyers on the *Whitford* side, in their amended complaint to the lower court, added Kagan's argument almost word for word, and also added more plaintiffs who could demonstrate individual harm in their own districts. Three federal judges were expected to hear the case again in Madison in July 2019. But on June 27, 2019, the US Supreme Court rejected the arguments about partisan gerrymandering in two related cases in North Carolina and Maryland and made a sweeping ruling that partisan gerrymandering should not be remedied by the federal courts.

"We conclude that partisan gerrymandering claims present political questions beyond the reach of the federal courts," chief justice John Roberts wrote. "Federal judges have no license to reallocate political power between the two major political parties, with no plausible grant of authority in the Constitution, and no legal standards to limit and direct their decisions." This, despite the fact that Roberts acknowledged that partisan gerrymandering was "incompatible with democratic principles."

Kagan, writing for the four liberals on the court, dissented bluntly. Gerrymandering, she said, is "anti-democratic in the most profound sense," and the types of partisan gerrymandering presented to the court in the North Carolina and Maryland cases "imperil our system of government. Part of the Court's role in that system is to defend its foundations. None is more important than free and fair elections."

As a result of this decision, the Wisconsin case could not move forward. The plaintiffs withdrew, and the *Whitford* case came to a close.

The only relief from the gerrymandering of 2011 came in a decision called *Baldus v. Brennan*, where a federal court ruled that two Wisconsin assembly districts in the predominantly Latino area of Milwaukee had been intentionally splintered to dilute their representation. That decision highlighted the interconnectedness of racial gerrymandering and hyperpartisan gerrymandering.

"Racial gerrymandering continues to happen, only masked as partisan gerrymandering," said Deborah Turner, president of the League of Women Voters of the United States, in a panel discussion she hosted in the fall of 2020 titled "Racism and Redistricting: How Unfair Maps Impact Communities of Color."

On that panel, Michael Futrell, a former member of Virginia's House of Delegates and now president of the National Black Nonpartisan Redistricting Organization, noted how gerrymandering leads to disengagement. "So many black and brown people say, 'My vote doesn't even count and even matter,' and the reason they feel like that is that they've been packed into districts that are 60, 70 percent, almost 80 percent" persons of color, he said. "Because you have packed so many into one district, in the neighboring districts where we could have a voice as well, we don't have a say, so our voices and our votes become diluted."

SOLUTIONS

Some political observers used to believe that the issue of gerrymandering was too obscure for most folks to grasp, too remote for the average citizen to care about. But the good news is that this is no longer the case in Wisconsin because an amazing grassroots movement has taken hold across the state to ban partisan gerrymandering.

Hans Breitenmoser is a dairy farmer near Merrill, a small city north of Wausau. His parents moved to the farm from Switzerland in 1968. "My mother says I was farming before I was born," he says. "She'd climb the silo while pregnant and fork out the silage. I was farming in utero." Breitenmoser now has 450 dairy cows, and despite the nasty downturn in the dairy market, he's managed to keep his operation going.

A Democrat on the Lincoln County Board of Supervisors, Breitenmoser maintains good relationships with his colleagues from both parties. Over time, he and other supervisors noticed that they weren't able to accomplish what they wanted because the Republican leadership in Madison had taken away so much local control. This frustration led Breitenmoser to the gerrymandering issue.

"At the county board level, we were feeling like things were getting worse and worse as far as the state was treating the county," he recalls. "I wondered, What's the disconnect here? If people want good roads and are willing to pay for them—and want good schools and are willing to pay for them—then why aren't we getting what we want?"

His answer? "We're not getting what we want because we're not placing people in office who rightly and fairly should be there. The disconnect is a symptom of having gerrymandered districts, and it's by design."

So Breitenmoser called our office at the Wisconsin Democracy Campaign one afternoon in January 2017, asking for information about how to combat gerrymandering and wondering how he might introduce a resolution to the county board in opposition to it.

We helped him with some wording, as did Jay Heck over at Common Cause Wisconsin, and Breitenmoser got the resolution passed on March 21, 2017, by a vote of 18–4.

But he wasn't content to stop there.

"I looked at Lincoln County as a means to an end, not an end in and of itself," he said. "Once we passed it, I was kind of excited, and I wanted to spread the word and inspire other people to do what we'd done. The fact that we passed it in Lincoln County—a small, red, rural county—was going to surprise some people. We expect stuff like this from Dane County, but for podunk Lincoln County to do it, it carried more weight."

Breitenmoser got in touch with supervisors in other counties, and, with help from grassroots groups like Citizen Action, other county boards began to take up the issue.

Breitenmoser also pressed the Wisconsin Counties Association, at its annual meeting in the Dells that September, to pass a resolution urging the state legislature to adopt nonpartisan gerrymandering. That resolution passed overwhelmingly.

By the end of 2020, fifty-four out of the seventy-two counties in Wisconsin had passed county board resolutions in favor of banning gerrymandering. Most of those are red counties, and most of them came on board just in the previous three years. In addition, twenty-eight counties have passed advisory referendums, by overwhelming margins, in favor of banning gerrymandering.

This is a testament not only to Breitenmoser's tenacity but also to an impressive united effort by progressive nonprofit groups, former elected officials, and grassroots activists to bring the issue of gerrymandering to the fore.

In 2017, the Wisconsin Fair Maps Coalition was formed, and it consisted primarily of Citizen Action of Wisconsin, Common Cause Wisconsin, the Wisconsin Fair Elections Project (which brought the *Whitford* lawsuit), League of Women Voters of Wisconsin, Wisconsin Democracy Campaign, and Wisconsin Voices. All these groups strategized together and worked harmoniously to publicize the issue. They were aided by two former senate majority leaders—Democrat Tim Cullen and Republican Dale Schultz—who traveled the state tirelessly, giving talks in one community after another about the need for fair maps in Wisconsin.

Other groups joined in along the way, including Play Fair Wisconsin, Our Wisconsin Revolution, Oregon Area Progressives, Unite America, Voces de la Frontera, Wisconsin Farmers Union, and Wisconsin United to Amend. Meanwhile, activists spontaneously arose to help out the effort all across the state.

Also providing key leadership was then state senator Dave Hansen of Green Bay, who introduced legislation in several sessions to give us independent, nonpartisan redistricting, along with representatives Don Vruwink and Robyn Vining.

And in January 2020, representative Dianne Hesselbein introduced a state constitutional amendment to ban gerrymandering and to ensure nonpartisan redistricting. Her proposal was cosponsored by representatives Jodi Emerson and Mark Spreitzer and senator Jeff Smith.

"Voters should choose their politicians; politicians should not choose their voters," said Hesselbein when she introduced her amendment. "If the people of Wisconsin pass this constitutional amendment, no political party will unfairly rig district maps in their favor ever again."

Here's one way I know that the issue has caught on. Before the COVID-19 pandemic, we would table at the Dane County Farmers' Market on the Square in Madison. We're stationed across from Park Bank and Genna's, and I stand in the grass and hector people as they pass by to sign our petition to ban gerrymandering. (I'm not a passive tabler.) We get more than three hundred signatures in two hours, and if you've ever tried to get signatures on any petition, you know that's not easy.

This mass movement is not going away. People are sick and tired of politicians manipulating the system for their own advantage, and gerrymandering is a prime example of this odious practice.

And it has odious consequences.

The first consequence is a lack of competitive races. As Spencer Black suggested, this makes the general election irrelevant, and the only election that matters then is the primary.

Lack of competitiveness leads to elected officials being able to ignore large swaths of their constituents. In a safe seat, an elected official can be unresponsive toward, and even disdainful of, his or her voters.

Lack of competitiveness also leads to hyperpartisanship. Elected officials can be as dogmatic as they would like because they won't pay any price for it. And in fact, if they don't toe the partisan line, their leader can threaten to "primary" them: threatening their political career by funding another candidate to run against them in the next primary—a candidate who would be more in lockstep. In such a climate, compromise becomes nearly impossible, and even plain old courtesy goes out the window.

Ultimately, gerrymandering leads to the people not getting what they want, whether that is an increase in Medicaid spending, more money for public education, medical marijuana, or a host of other vastly popular items—including banning gerrymandering itself.

The people of Wisconsin have had enough of the trickery, and the unresponsiveness, and the disdain, and the rudeness that gerrymandering engenders. They want basic fairness and a level playing field.

According to a Marquette University Law School poll in January 2019, 72 percent of Wisconsinites want independent, nonpartisan map drawing. And that includes 63 percent of Republicans and 76 percent of Independents.

Candidates and elected officials who ignore the overwhelming will of the people on this issue will at some point pay a price—yes, even in their gerrymandered districts.

Other states, even Utah and Missouri, are banning gerrymandering. It's long past time Wisconsin did so too.

COUNTERARGUMENTS AND COMPLEXITIES

It's Unconstitutional

Republican leaders in the legislature contend that adopting a version of the Iowa model of independent, nonpartisan redistricting would be unconstitutional. They claim that the Wisconsin Constitution requires elected officials—and not members of the Legislative Reference Bureau (LRB), the nonpartisan agency of career civil servants who aid the legislature—to draw the maps.

Of course, in 2011, it wasn't legislators who drew the maps. Staffers for the Speaker and the majority leader and a political scientist from Oklahoma drew them.

Leaving that aside, let's take a look at the Wisconsin Constitution. Article IV, Section 3, requires that "at their first session after each enumeration made by the authority of the United States, the legislature shall apportion and district anew the members of the senate and assembly, according to the number of inhabitants."

Under the Iowa model, the legislature would still be doing the apportioning and redistricting, since its members would be the ones voting on the maps presented by the staff of the LRB, just as they voted on the maps presented to them in 2011.

We Can't Rely on "Bureaucrats"

Speaker Vos sneered at the whole idea of letting career civil servants draw the maps. He belittled them as "bureaucrats," saying he wasn't going to hand "over our constitutional duty to an unelected, unaccountable board of bureaucrats."

The attack on "bureaucrats" is an oldy-moldy that demagogues like to toss around, but our government relies on civil service workers to get things done. And under the Iowa model, as I've noted, the members of the LRB would be required by law not to use political demographic data to tilt the maps in favor of one party or another. It is this requirement that sticks in the craw of the Speaker, not the fact that the staff of the LRB would be drawing the maps, because if you can't use past voting patterns in each district when you're redrawing the maps, the only way you can rig the maps is by guesswork.

The Democrats "Self-Pack"

Wisconsin Republicans also argue that gerrymandering isn't the reason that they hold a large majority in the legislature. Instead, it's because Democrats "self-pack": most of them choose to reside in Milwaukee or Madison, which leaves fertile ground everywhere else in Wisconsin for Republicans to dominate.

While it's certainly true that a lot of Democrats congregate in Madison and Milwaukee, Republicans also "self-pack" in Waukesha, Ozaukee, and Washington Counties.

What's more, and what decisively destroys this argument, is the fact that the Republican leadership went to extraordinary lengths in 2011 to redraw districts all over the state, not just in Dane and Milwaukee Counties. They were moving lines everywhere, manipulating district boundaries far from these Democratic strongholds!

Nonpartisan Gerrymandering Is Bad for Democrats!

Here's an argument from Jonathan Rodden, a Stanford political scientist, who lays it out in his book *Why Cities Lose*. Basically, he acknowledges that Democrats self-pack in large urban areas and concludes that this disadvantages their ability to get equal representation.

"The clustering of Democrats in cities often provides Republican map-drawers with an excellent starting point, such that they could achieve a disproportionate seat share without much effort or skill—simply by drawing compact and contiguous districts, as the law often demands," he writes.

Rodden takes the logic of his argument to the extreme, advising Democrats to do some clever gerrymandering of their own. "While gerrymandering has allowed Republicans to build upon their geographic advantage, in some states," he writes, "artful gerrymandering might also be the only way for Democrats to overcome that advantage. While many Democrats like the idea of a party-blind redistricting process that produces geometrically compact districts, such a process would actually be quite beneficial to the Republicans in a number of competitive states."

Fred Kessler, a former judge and Democratic assembly member who was one of the prime movers behind taking the *Whitford* case to the US Supreme Court, is not as blunt as Rodden. But Kessler agrees that blind nonpartisan redistricting will not give Wisconsin equal representation. Kessler notes that the state has been essentially evenly divided over the last four or five presidential races, and yet the legislature has tilted decisively toward the Republicans.

Kessler doesn't believe that the Iowa model provides enough newly competitive districts to accurately reflect the purple makeup of Wisconsin's electorate in the legislature. And so he wants to throw out a couple of the key elements of the Iowa model to arrive at more competitive districts.

First, he argues, we actually need to use political demographic data. "If election data is not included in the formulation considered, there is no realistic possibility that a fair legislative map will be prepared," he wrote in an eight-page memo in 2020.

Second, he says, we need to get over our affection for natural or traditional boundaries. "Compactness, contiguousness, and preservation of local and county lines are usually required in statutory and constitutional provisions," he writes. But to get to really competitive districts, he says, "you would have to draw the map disregarding city and county boundaries."

But I'm not at all convinced, by either Rodden or Kessler, that Democrats or progressives should do some "artful gerrymandering" of their own if they ever get the chance. Quite the contrary! This is anathema to me, as it is to most people in the Wisconsin movement to ban gerrymandering.

Yes, I suppose Democrats could, if they were in total control, take a tiny section of west Madison and run it into Iowa County, and then take a slice of east Madison and run it up into Columbia County, and take a slice of the

Isthmus all the way down to Walworth County, but again, it's wrong when Republicans gerrymander, and it's wrong when Democrats gerrymander.

There are other ways to address the problem of self-packing. Rodden suggests having larger districts, for one thing. He also proposes proportional representation, where each party receives a number of seats based on its share of the vote.

But those reforms are a long way off, and I'm prepared to accept the problem of self-packing as the lesser of two evils.

The only exception I would allow to the rule about "compactness" and "contiguousness" would be to authorize the map drawers to honor communities of interest. These consist of well-defined racial, ethnic, cultural, social, linguistic, and economic communities that have a legitimate claim on representation. But other than that, don't monkey with the map.

chapter 2

Reform Campaign Finance

On Friday night, November 6, 2015, I was almost alone in the gallery of the Wisconsin Senate Chamber. Only a Capitol Police officer and a young senate page were up there with me. Down below, we were witnessing a disaster for democracy: The Republicans were ripping apart Wisconsin's campaign finance law (which ironically is called Chapter 11) from top to bottom.

Starting at the top, they were determined to strike even the high-minded rhetoric that prefaced the old law. That "Declaration of Policy" said, among other things, that "our democratic system of government can be maintained only if the electorate is informed" and that "excessive spending on campaigns for public office jeopardizes the integrity of elections."

It also noted that "when the true source of support or extent of support is not fully disclosed, or when a candidate becomes overly dependent upon large private contributors, the democratic process is subjected to a potential corrupting influence."

And it concluded that "the state has a compelling interest in designing a system for fully disclosing contributions and disbursements made on behalf of every candidate for public office, and in placing reasonable limitations on such activities."

But the Republicans in the senate would have none of such niceties and stripped them all out.

Democratic senators introduced an amendment to try to save that lofty rhetoric.

"Restore the language!" demanded senator Mark Miller.

"Why do you want to take it out?" asked senator Fred Risser, the longest-sitting legislator in American history. "This is a good part of our tradition. You ought to read it. You ought to live by it."

But out it went—tabled on a party-line vote, 18–14.

When they got down to the substantive changes to the law, the Republicans did even more damage.

First, they doubled the amount that rich individuals in Wisconsin could give to their favorite candidates. For instance, the old law said that the most you could give to someone running for governor was $10,000 (itself a ridiculously high amount). But under the new law, now rich and poor alike in Wisconsin can write a check for $20,000 to their favorite candidate for governor.

Second, they tore down the de facto $10,000 ceiling on individual donations to political parties. Wisconsin used to have an aggregate limit of $10,000 on individual donations. So if you gave $10,000 to Scott Walker for Governor, you couldn't give a dime to the Republican Party of Wisconsin or to any state senate or state assembly candidate. The US Supreme Court's *McCutcheon v. FEC* decision in 2014 said that aggregate limits were unconstitutional, so Wisconsin's $10,000 aggregate limit had to go. The state senate could have reimposed a $10,000 ceiling on donations to political parties if it wanted to. But it chose not to.

As a result, superrich individuals have been writing seven-figure checks to the Republican Party of Wisconsin and the Democratic Party of Wisconsin. And not all those checks have come from Wisconsinites. One came from Omaha, Nebraska. The check, to the Republican Party of Wisconsin, was written by Marlene Ricketts, who lives in Omaha—and even more galling to Brewers fans, she's a co-owner of the Chicago Cubs. Another came from Karla Jurvetson, a doctor in Los Altos, California, who gave to the Democratic Party of Wisconsin. And Illinois governor J. B. Pritzker gave the Democrats $2.49 million. (The superrich on both sides are playing the big money game in Wisconsin.)

Third, the Republicans tore down the limits on how much political parties could give to candidates for state senate and assembly. Prior to 2015, senate candidates could receive no more than $22,435 from PACs and political parties combined, and assembly candidates could receive no more than $11,213. But under the current law, there is no limit. The sky is the limit. This change, in combination with tearing down the ceiling on individual donations to the political parties, means that superrich individuals can give obscene amounts to the political parties, which can then turn around and give those amounts to the candidates, even though the amounts might be one hundred times the legal limit on what an individual could give directly to the candidates. This turns the political parties into glorified laundromats.

Fourth, Republican legislators let corporations—for the first time in more than one hundred years—contribute directly to political parties. They said those donations could not exceed $12,000 and they required those donations to be put in "segregated" accounts that were not supposed to be used directly on campaigns. But such funds are fungible and can be used to pay for staff salaries and overhead, which frees up other funds for campaigning, so it's a distinction that doesn't make a difference.

Poor Fighting Bob La Follette! He spent his life trying to combat corporate contamination of our politics here in Wisconsin. This change in our campaign finance law must have spun him around in his grave at warp speed.

Fifth, the Republicans let corporations give those same $12,000 checks to the four legislative campaign committees that are run, respectively, by the Speaker of the assembly, the minority leader of the assembly, the majority leader of the senate, and the minority leader of the senate. And they let individuals give unlimited amounts to these committees. These changes greatly enhanced the power of these leaders. They now have vastly more resources at their disposal, and they can use those resources to keep any wayward legislator of their own party in line. Any legislator who strays can now be "primaried." The legislative leader will say, "If you step out of line, I'm going to get someone to run against you in the primary, and I've got a big pile of money here that'll destroy you." That's the kind of language most politicians understand.

And sixth, Republicans let candidates coordinate with dark money groups, placing into the statutes the same permission slip that the Wisconsin Supreme Court provided when it ended the *John Doe II* case (more about that case in chapter 6). So now, unless an outside group uses the words "vote for" or "vote against" a specific person, the candidate can work with that group. This makes a mockery of the whole idea of setting limits on individual donations to candidates and on the necessity of full disclosure.

Let me explain. Say I'm running for governor, and I've got a billionaire friend who wants to help me in secret and who wants to do business with the State of Wisconsin. I'm going to say, "Well, you could write me a check for $20,000 but I'd have to disclose that so I got a better idea. Write a check for $2 million to this group I control. It's got a sweet-sounding name: Badgers for Eternal Victory. Write the check out to BEV, and I'll tell BEV how to put that money to good use. I'll even write the TV script, and I'll tell BEV which stations to run it on. And the script will say something like, 'The other candidate for governor is a bum. Call him at (608) He-Sucks and tell him to stop acting like such a bum. This ad was paid for by Badgers for Eternal Victory.'" It's all perfectly legal now. It'll be like you gave my campaign the money, but you gave me a hundred times what you could have directly, and the kicker is that BEV doesn't have to disclose that you gave it a single dime.

I might also tell my billionaire friend, "If you want to spread it around, you could give another $2 million to whichever political party in the state that I belong to, and that party can then shovel that money back to my campaign, no questions asked."

You can bet that if I got elected, my friend would receive preferential treatment for all his largesse.

Finally, Republicans required less disclosure in another way. They got rid of the old requirement that campaigns list the employer of donors who gave $100 or more. Now all they have to do is list the occupation of the donor—such as businessperson. Well, there are tens of thousands of people who might fall in that category, so that doesn't give you a clue about whether the specific business the donor works for is getting something on the back side in return for a big donation.

Democratic senators tried to raise some of these objections as the night wore on. "Your changes to campaign finance law will only serve to increase the amount of corporate and dark money coming in from out of state and out of the country," said senator Dave Hansen. "Pay to play and political corruption like we're used to reading about in states like Illinois, New Jersey, and Florida won't be far behind. In the meantime, voters are going to be even angrier once they see that they can't turn on their TV, answer their phones, or go to their mailboxes without being inundated with more and more negative ads."

"We as legislators are going to be very bit players," said senator Jon Erpenbach. "We'll be drowned out by all the money coming in. . . . You are minimizing your role as a candidate because the big money powerbrokers are going to have all the say in this state."

Erpenbach was especially incensed that "there isn't disclosure when it comes to issue advocacy groups." He made up the names of some such groups, saying that we'll never know where the money is coming from when groups like Friends for a Sunny Day, We Love Cheese, or How 'Bout Them Packers start running their dark money ads. "This piece of legislation is going to allow millions and millions more unregulated, unaccounted for, money," he warned.

Senate minority leader Jen Shilling herself made the point that this new law was turning legislative leaders into kingmakers. "You better stay on the side of your legislative leader because they're going to have tremendous power," she said. "Be forewarned. Stay on that good side because they will have tremendous amount of power and access to move this money around."

Senator Tim Carpenter echoed this point: "You're going to have to kiss the rings of people in leadership. . . . After this bill passes, and you say no to leadership, you can be replaced."

Senator Chris Larson said, "This is one of the darkest days of Wisconsin, as more collusion is allowed in our state, as more cash is allowed in elections, and more corruption is allowed in our halls."

Toward midnight, the bill passed, 17–15, with only one Republican voting against it: senator Rob Cowles from the Green Bay area. In the *Wisconsin State Journal*, Cowles told the reporter he's always been against more money in politics, just like his mother. "She hated the garbage of politics," Cowles said. "The mass mailings, the stupid TV ads, the fluff, all of that is propelled by this bill."

Sometimes, we do the right thing because our parents are still whispering in our ears, often even after they're dead.

The need for campaign finance reform couldn't be more urgent. And here's one more reason for that urgency: our current system, which so favors the superwealthy and the big corporations, discriminates against people of color. Campaign finance reform is a civil rights issue.

This is all spelled out in a 2015 report from the nonprofit group Demos, "Stacked Deck: How the Racial Bias in Our Big Money Political System Undermines Our Democracy and Our Economy." As the report states: "The undemocratic role of big money is especially exclusionary for people of color, who are severely underrepresented in the 'donor class' whose large contributions fuel campaigns and therefore set the agendas in Washington and state capitals across the country."

A couple of years ago, the Wisconsin Democracy Campaign listed the top fifty donors to Republican candidates in Wisconsin and the top fifty donors to Democratic candidates in Wisconsin, and only one of the one hundred donors was a minority: Richard Abdoo, the former CEO of Wisconsin Energy Corporation, who is an Arab American.

"Because donor and corporate interests often diverge significantly from those of working families on economic policies such as the minimum wage and paid sick leave, people of color are disproportionately harmed because a larger percentage are poor or working class," the Demos report noted. "The dominance of big money in our politics makes it far harder for people of color to exert political power and effectively advocate for their interests as both wealth and power are consolidated by a small, very white, share of the population."

SOLUTIONS

There are solutions to the problem of money in politics, and fortunately there are prodemocracy legislators, nonprofit groups, and activists in Wisconsin propelling these solutions forward.

On Valentine's Day 2019, Senator Larson held a sparsely attended press conference in the Senate Parlor to introduce his "Campaign Integrity Package." That package would undo most of the damage that was inflicted by the Republican legislature back on that November evening in 2015.

"Powerful special interest groups and wealthy corporations continue to have an overwhelming and growing effect on elections across Wisconsin and nationwide," Larson said.

Several of Larson's bills would reduce the amount that individuals can give directly to candidates, political parties, legislative campaign committees, and PACs.

Two bills would ban corporations, unions, tribes, and other groups from giving to political parties and legislative campaign committees.

Another bill would ban coordination between candidates and "issue advocacy" groups.

And three bills would bring more transparency. One would require "issue advocacy" groups that engage in electioneering to disclose the names of their donors who give $100 or more. Another would require campaigns to list the employer of any donor who gives $100 or more. And a third bill would plug a loophole in the law that allows most national PACs not to register with, or disclose their donors to, the State of Wisconsin.

These are all doable reforms. But we need to go further. The amounts that individuals and groups are allowed to give should be even lower. The old limits on individual donations for governor or Wisconsin Supreme Court justice were $10,000. Who's got ten grand to throw around? We should also empower small donors by matching their donations with public funds, as other places are doing. For instance, Seattle offers its citizens four $25 vouchers to use in each mayoral election. And New York City has a public financing system whereby, if a candidate accepts expenditure limits, the small donors to that candidate will have their donations (up to $175) matched at a 6:1 ratio by public funds. So if you give $100 to your candidate, the city gives that candidate an extra $600.

Ultimately we need full public financing of elections in Wisconsin—and nationally. But to get to where we need to be, though, we're going to have to topple the whole edifice of US Supreme Court decisions that magically transformed corporations into persons and money into speech with the wave of a gavel. These decisions go as far back as *Santa Clara County v. Southern Pacific Railroad* (1886), where an employee of the high court inserted a head note on the decision that said that "corporations are persons." None of the justices wrote that, but it became part of the decision and was cited as precedent in subsequent Supreme Court rulings. Ever since then, right through *Buckley v. Valeo* in 1976 and *Citizens United* in 2010 and onward, Supreme Court decisions have been amplifying the voices of corporations and the wealthy and muffling the voices of regular flesh-and-blood citizens.

There's a growing movement around the country to amend the US Constitution to proclaim, once and for all, that corporations aren't persons and money isn't speech. And I'm happy to report that Wisconsin activists are helping to lead the way. Thanks to some amazing organizing by the all-volunteer folks at Wisconsin United to Amend, 166 communities in Wisconsin had passed resolutions or referendums by the end of 2020 avowing their support for this crucial amendment. This makes Wisconsin second only to Massachusetts in having the most communities on board. I believe this crucial amendment to the US Constitution will pass in the next ten to fifteen years. Only then will we, the citizens of Wisconsin and the citizens of the United States, have anywhere close to an equal say over who gets elected and what laws are passed and what policies are pursued.

By the way, at Larson's press conference, I read a little valentine that I had composed for the occasion. It went like this:

Dear Democracy in Wisconsin,
Won't you be my valentine?
I love you!
But I'm worried about you.
And I want you to get your act together.
You've let the superwealthy and the big corporations take over the funding of
    our elections, drowning out the voices of the rest of us.
Democracy, you can barely hear us now.
Democracy, you're drowning in dark money.
Democracy, don't let them sully your name any longer.
So take this bouquet of bills from Senator Larson and, on this Valentine's Day,
    together let us celebrate our mutual love of clean and open government,
    where everyone has an equal voice.
Happy Valentine's Day!

COUNTERARGUMENTS AND COMPLEXITIES

Wisconsin's Law Needed to Be Rewritten because of US Supreme Court Decisions

This is certainly true. Several US Supreme Court decisions had rendered the Wisconsin campaign finance chapter obsolete. Chief among them:

- *Wisconsin Right to Life v. FEC* in 2007, which said that so-called issue advocacy groups—those that don't use the magic words "vote for" or "vote against" a particular candidate—didn't have to disclose their donors, who could spend unlimited amounts to fund these dark money ads.
- *Citizens United* in 2010, which said that corporations, unions, and other groups could spend unlimited amounts of money telling you who to vote for or vote against so long as they don't coordinate their activities with the candidate they are supporting. This gave rise to the super-PACs, where the twenty-five richest individuals in the country have spent more than $2 billion on electioneering ads in the decade following the decision.
- *McCutcheon v. FEC* in 2014, which said that there can be no aggregate limits on how much an individual can give during a political season. Wisconsin, as I mentioned, had a $10,000 aggregate limit.

Despite these adverse and antidemocratic rulings from the high court, none of these rulings required the Republican legislature and Governor Walker to do the following:

- double the limits that individuals can give directly to candidates
- tear down the de facto $10,000 limit on individual donations to political parties
- tear down the same de facto limit on individual donations to legislative campaign committees
- allow corporations to give directly to political parties and legislative campaign committees
- remove the requirement that donors who give more than $100 have to disclose who they work for.

So, yes, rulings by the US Supreme Court required a reworking of our campaign finance statute, but they didn't require most of the disastrous changes that gave the wealthy and corporations more power than they've had in a century to influence Wisconsin's politics.

Restrictions on Political Spending Infringe on Free Speech

The other counterarguments and complexities in this chapter relate not specifically to Wisconsin's campaign finance law but to the constitutional questions themselves.

Here's the core counterargument: restrictions on political spending by corporations or individuals are infringements on political speech.

But even the US Supreme Court—in a series of decisions from *Buckley v. Valeo* in 1976 through *Wisconsin Right to Life* and *Citizens United* and *McCutcheon*, as well as *Caperton v. Massey Coal* (2009)—hasn't gone that far out on this shaky First Amendment limb. No, it crawled back toward the trunk of democracy by noting that limits on some campaign money—specifically, direct donations to candidates—are permissible to avoid corruption or the appearance of it.

But the high court has drawn that line too narrowly, focusing on "quid pro quo" corruption and letting everything else go. This led to a profound dissent, in *Wisconsin Right to Life*, from justice David Souter: "Neither Congress's decisions nor our own have understood the corrupting influence of money in politics as being limited to outright bribery or discrete *quid pro quo*; campaign finance reform has instead consistently focused on the more pervasive distortion of electoral institutions by concentrated wealth, on the special access and guaranteed favor that sap the representative integrity of American government and defy public confidence in its institutions."

Justice John Paul Stevens, in a blistering and prophetic dissent in *Citizens United*, assailed the high court's reasoning across the board. First, he eviscerated the claim that corporations are persons:

> The conceit that corporations must be treated identically to natural persons in the political sphere is not only inaccurate but also inadequate to justify the Court's disposition of this case. . . . The financial resources, legal structure, and instrumental orientation of corporations raise legitimate concerns about their role in the electoral process. Our lawmakers have a compelling constitutional basis, if not also a democratic duty, to take measures designed to guard against the potentially deleterious effects of corporate spending in local and national races. . . . Corporations have no consciences, no beliefs, no feelings, no thoughts, no desires. Corporations help structure and facilitate the activities of human beings, to be sure, and their "personhood" often serves as a useful legal fiction. But they are not themselves members of "We the People" by whom and for whom our Constitution was established.

Then he went after the parched claim that outlaws only quid pro quo contributions:

> On numerous occasions we have recognized Congress' legitimate interest in preventing the money that is spent on elections from exerting an "'undue influence on an officeholder's judgment'" and from creating "'the appearance of such influence,'" beyond the sphere of *quid pro quo* relationships. [citations omitted] Corruption can take many forms. Bribery may be the paradigm case. But the difference between selling a vote and selling access is a matter of degree, not kind. And selling access is not qualitatively different from giving special preference to those who spent money on one's behalf. Corruption operates along a spectrum, and the majority's apparent belief that *quid pro quo* arrangements can be neatly demarcated from other improper influences does not accord with the theory or reality of politics.

He warned that corporations would now find it much easier to get whatever they want from our elected officials: "Starting today, corporations with large war chests to deploy on electioneering may find democratically elected bodies becoming much more attuned to their interests." He added that the court's decision "will undoubtedly cripple the ability of ordinary citizens, Congress, and the States to adopt even limited measures to protect against corporate domination of the electoral process. Americans may be forgiven if they do not feel the Court has advanced the cause of self-government today."

He also hurled a couple of First Amendment arguments of his own. One argument was that allowing unlimited corporate speech muffles the voices of ordinary citizens. "The opinions of real people may be marginalized . . . [by the] immediate drowning out of non-corporate voices," he wrote. He added that it's not only the vast amounts of money at the hands of corporations that drowns out individuals, but also the ease by which the corporations can throw their money around, whereas individuals would have to seek out other like-minded individuals to try to mount a response, and that's much harder than simply dipping into the corporate treasury.

Another argument Stevens raised was that by drowning out the voices of ordinary people, corporate speech deprives citizens of the First Amendment right to listen to others:

> The majority seems oblivious to the simple truth that laws such as [the McCain-Feingold] do not merely pit the anticorruption interest against the First Amendment, but also pit competing First Amendment values against each other. There are, to be sure, serious concerns with any effort to balance the First Amendment rights of speakers against the First Amendment rights of listeners. But when the speakers in question are not real people and when the appeal to "First Amendment principles" depends almost entirely on the listeners' perspective, it becomes necessary to consider how listeners will actually be affected.

In this regard, Stevens was echoing the dissent of justice Thurgood Marshall in *Kleindienst v. Mandel* (1972), who wrote: "The freedom to speak and the freedom to hear are inseparable; they are two sides of the same coin."

In short, the US Supreme Court has itself recognized the need to limit some political speech. And there are competing First Amendment claims, as well as competing democracy claims, that make the compelling case for limiting corporate political speech and excessive spending by individuals in political campaigns.

What about the Media Exemption?

In *Citizens United*, the majority tried to put proponents of regulating corporate speech in a box, essentially by arguing that if you believe the government should be able to limit or ban the ability of corporations to tell you who to vote for or vote against, are you saying the media should be banned from making endorsements? They are corporations, after all. And if you include them, then what about the First Amendment's protection for freedom of the press?

Advocates for limiting corporate spending in campaigns acknowledged that the media were exempt, so this prompted the conservatives on the court to retort:

> The exemption applies to media corporations owned or controlled by corporations that have diverse and substantial investments and participate in endeavors other than news. So even assuming the most doubtful proposition that a news organization has a right to speak when others do not, the exemption would allow a conglomerate that owns both a media business and an unrelated business to influence or control the media in order to advance its overall business interest. At the same time, some other corporation, with an identical business interest but no media outlet in its ownership structure, would be forbidden to speak or inform the public about the same issue. This differential treatment cannot be squared with the First Amendment.

To complete the trap, the majority wrote in the next sentence: "There is simply no support for the view that the First Amendment, as originally understood, would permit the suppression of political speech by media corporations."

Certainly, the last point is correct: the First Amendment's freedom of the press clause would forbid the banning of endorsements by media corporations. So, yes, there is an element of unfairness here. But that unfairness is far better than just letting all corporations dip into their treasury and fling money at candidates they like—and mud at those they don't—and drown out the rest of us.

What's more, it's an unfairness that comports with the Founders' belief in the unique role of the press. As justice Potter Stewart put it, the media is "the only organized private business that is given explicit constitutional protection." Stevens, in his *Citizens United* dissent, echoed this, stressing "the unique role played by the institutional press in sustaining public debate."

Stevens also noted that this unfairness is mitigated by the fact that the media actors are out in the open for all to see, including their stockholders, whereas other kinds of companies could throw their weight around on the sly. "With a media corporation there is also a lesser risk that investors will not understand, learn about, or support the advocacy messages that the corporation disseminates," Stevens wrote.

Lawrence Lessig's Apostasy

One of the leading advocates of prodemocracy reforms over the past twenty years has been professor Lawrence Lessig of Harvard Law School. In his latest book, *They Don't Represent Us: Reclaiming Our Democracy*, he takes the heretical position that we shouldn't be able to regulate corporate spending—with one major exception—in our elections.

"Should the spending of a corporation be limited? This is not a popular view with my tribe, but I don't think, in general, that difference matters" between whether an individual is doing the spending or a corporation, he writes. "The constitutional question is not 'who is speaking.' The constitutional question is 'what kind of speech is this.' And if it is political speech, then the Constitution protects that speech as vigorously as it can."

I don't find Lessig's claim here persuasive in the least, since he hasn't bothered to wrestle with the various points raised by Stevens as to why corporations should not have the same free speech rights in the political arena as flesh-and-blood humans.

What's more, his own exception destroys his argument. Lessig says that we should be able to regulate the spending by super-PACs. Why super-PACS and not corporations? Lessig says that super-PACs undermine representative government. "First," he notes, "they have become hugely prominent in American political life. . . . That prominence, second, means that candidates are focused on—some might say, obsessed with—whether these SuperPACs will or will not support them." Our representatives, in short, are answering to the super-PACs, and not the people.

But the same could be said of large-scale corporate spending in our elections. It's becoming very prominent in our political life, and as it grows, candidates are becoming obsessed with that too. And once Lessig concedes that we have a compelling reason to curb super-PAC spending, he no longer has a principle to invoke to stop us from doing what Stevens says we should do: limit corporate spending in campaigns.

chapter 3

Make Voting Easier

It's August 22, 1980, in Dallas. The Religious Roundtable, a coalition of conservative Christians, is holding a gathering of some fifteen thousand people for a national affairs briefing that is featuring a speech by candidate Ronald Reagan. Leading up to Reagan's talk is Paul Weyrich, one of the founders of the social conservative movement. Weyrich doesn't mince his words.

First, he makes fun of people who advocate for good-government issues. "How many of our Christians have what I call the 'goo goo' syndrome?" he asks. "They want *everybody* to vote"—a ridiculous idea, according to Weyrich.

"I don't want everybody to vote," he bluntly tells the crowd. "As a matter of fact, our leverage in the elections, quite candidly, goes up as the voting population goes down."

Michael Waldman, head of the Brennan Center for Justice, relays this anecdote in his excellent book *The Fight to Vote*. Waldman and other scholars, such as Carol Anderson in *One Person, No Vote: How Voter Suppression Is Destroying Our Democracy*, have documented in great detail how, in state after state, conservative elected officials have made it harder—not easier—to vote.

In the Jim Crow era, voter suppression was carried out by violence, threats of violence, poll taxes, and ludicrous literacy tests. Black citizens who wanted to vote in the South had to answer such questions as how many bubbles are in a bar of soap or were given incomprehensible legal passages to decipher. The local white clerk had absolute discretion to say whether you passed the test or not.

In the modern era, voter suppression got a big boost from the US Supreme Court, in the *Shelby County v. Holder* case of 2013, which did away with part of the Voting Rights Act that had compelled many southern states to get pre-approval from the Justice Department before they could make any changes to their voting laws.

Justice Ruth Bader Ginsburg noted in her scathing dissent, which she read aloud: "The sad irony of today's decision lies in its utter failure to grasp why the [Voting Rights Act] has proven effective. . . . Throwing out pre-clearance when it has worked and is continuing to work to stop discriminatory changes is like throwing away your umbrella in a rainstorm because you are not getting wet."

Shortly after the *Shelby* decision came down, one southern state after another introduced voter suppression laws.

But Wisconsin, under governor Scott Walker, beat them to it. Walker and the GOP legislature passed their so-called voter ID law in 2011.

When it passed, Republican state senators were described by Todd Albaugh, chief of staff of Republican senator Dale Schultz, as being "giddy" that they were making it harder for minorities and young people to vote.

The voter ID law requires you to show a government-issued ID with your photo on it when you go to vote. It prohibits vouching, a formerly common practice in Wisconsin where a registered voter could corroborate the identity of a new voter. It also limited early voting from thirty days to twelve days and allowed only one location for early voting per municipality.

US district judge James Peterson, in *One Wisconsin Institute v. Thomsen* (2016), threw out the restrictions on early voting, saying they were designed to "suppress the reliably Democratic vote of Milwaukee's African-Americans." He added, "The Wisconsin experience demonstrates that a preoccupation with mostly phantom election fraud leads to real incidents of disenfranchisement, which undermine rather than enhance confidence in elections, particularly in minority communities. To put it bluntly, Wisconsin's strict version of voter ID law is a worse cure than the disease."

And then in the lame duck session in late 2018, Speaker Robin Vos and majority leader Scott Fitzgerald again tried to limit early voting, and Peterson again struck it down, for the same reason.

On June 29, 2020, in its outrageous decision in the *One Wisconsin Institute* case, a three-judge panel of the Seventh Circuit Court of Appeals in Chicago overruled Peterson and restored the twelve-day limit on early voting. The judges—all appointed by Republicans—said the voter ID law's limit on early voting was not about race but about "voters' political preferences." In essence, they said that the effort to curb the voting of Blacks in Milwaukee was not because they are Black but because they vote Democratic.

"If one party can make changes that it believes help its candidates, the other can restore the original rules or revise the new ones," the judges ruled. That statement is either embarrassingly disingenuous or hopelessly naive, because the party that's not in power has a much more difficult time gaining power after the rules have been rigged against it.

On top of limiting early voting, the voter ID law has put needless obstacles in the way of people getting to the voting booth. The problem with voter ID is that many young people, people of color, and elderly people don't have driver's licenses, the most common form of permissible IDs.

Going to the DMV to get an ID is not as easy as it seems if you're disabled or don't have a vehicle. And finding a DMV that's open can be tricky. For instance, if you lived in Sauk City in 2018, the DMV was open only on the fifth Wednesday of every month, and only four months had a fifth Wednesday!

The voter ID law also makes it especially difficult for Wisconsin college and university students who don't have in-state driver's licenses. Their college IDs work only if they include the student's name, signature, photo, date the card was issued, and the date the card expires (which can't be more than two years from the issuance date). What's more, the voter ID law requires students to show proof of current enrollment, such as a receipt for tuition paid.

These are "completely unnecessary hoops that the Wisconsin voter ID law forces students to jump through to be able to vote," says Jay Heck, director of Common Cause Wisconsin, which is suing the Wisconsin Elections Commission.

"Lacking an important regulatory interest to impose these redundant, unnecessary, and irrational requirements for college and university student ID cards which needlessly force students to obtain a different campus photo ID card in order to vote, Defendants violate the First and Fourteenth Amendments to the U.S. Constitution," the complaint argues.

The voter ID law has had its desired effect: Both Republican representative Glenn Grothman and Brad Schimel, a former attorney general of Wisconsin, said in public that this law helped or was going to help Republicans win elections in Wisconsin. In fact, it may have been a big reason that Trump carried Wisconsin in 2016, because a lot of voters were turned away at the polls or discouraged from voting by the voter ID law.

"Thousands, and perhaps tens of thousands, of otherwise eligible people were deterred from voting by the ID law," said UW–Madison political science professor Ken Mayer, who did a study of the issue. Poor and minority populations were affected the most, Mayer added.

Other voter suppression tactics were at play in 2016 in Wisconsin. "In 2016, the Trump campaign categorized 3.5 million Black Americans as voters they wanted to deter from participating in the election," wrote Brianna Reilly of the Madison *Capital Times* on October 14, 2020. "In Wisconsin, where Black people make up 5.4% of the population, they represented 17% of those categorized for 'Deterrence.'"

Angela Lang, executive director of Black Leaders Organizing for Communities, told Reilly that this puts the lie to Republican outreach to the Black community: "It just goes to show that all of the campaign promises, all of the records that they try to tout about how great they've been for our community, it's really disingenuous now because you don't actively want our vote. You're actually trying to suppress it."

Another effort to suppress the vote in Wisconsin came in the fall of 2019 when the right-wing Wisconsin Institute for Law and Liberty (WILL) filed a lawsuit against the Wisconsin Elections Commission to force it to drop 234,000 citizens from the voter rolls who hadn't responded within thirty days to a mailing from the commission asking to verify their addresses. The mailing, however, didn't notify them that they would be dropped from the rolls if they didn't respond.

Circuit court judge Paul Malloy sided with WILL and ordered the names immediately purged. The order wasn't enforced, however, because a three-judge appellate panel overturned that decision and the Wisconsin Supreme Court deadlocked on the issue.

Had the purge gone into effect, it would have targeted Black voters, says the prodemocracy group Demos, since "a disproportionate number of mailers were sent to areas with large Black voting bases." The *Wisconsin State Journal* (December 26, 2019) noted that "about 35,343 registered voters in Milwaukee could see their registrations revoked" (Milwaukee has the highest percentage of Black voters in Wisconsin).

Conservatives were just warming up. In late November 2019, Justin Clark, a senior campaign aide to Donald Trump, came to Wisconsin to boast about voter suppression. "Traditionally, it's always been Republicans suppressing votes" in battleground states like Wisconsin, he told a group of Republican leaders, adding: "Let's start playing offense a little bit. That's what you're going to see in 2020. It's going to be a much bigger program, a much more aggressive program, a much better funded program."

Then came the debacle during the 2020 spring elections, right at one of the worst periods of the coronavirus pandemic. After dilly-dallying for weeks about whether to postpone the election or not, governor Tony Evers, who had issued an emergency declaration and ordered Wisconsinites to stay home, finally urged legislators to push the election. The Republicans, in control of both the assembly and the senate, refused. Evers called them into special session the Saturday before the scheduled April 7 vote, which Republicans summarily gaveled in and gaveled out in three seconds' time, with no discussion or debate.

Finally, the day before the election, Evers issued an executive ordering postponing the election until June 9. Speaker Vos and majority leader Fitzgerald immediately appealed to the Wisconsin Supreme Court, which ruled hours later, in a partisan 4–2 vote, that the election had to go on the following day.

Citizens who hadn't cast absentee ballots (or hadn't received them yet!) were forced to choose between surrendering their right to vote or risking their lives going to the polls during a lethal pandemic.

The outrageous decision to hold the primary election on April 7 was especially dicey for people in Milwaukee. Instead of the usual 180 polling places, only five were open for the entire city of some 600,000 people—240,000 of them Black. In addition, a coronavirus outbreak was affecting a disproportionate number of Blacks. Forcing Black Milwaukeeans into this voting trap was one of the most cynical and callous things I've ever seen in my entire life. And sure enough, the lines were two hours long in Milwaukee, and it was difficult to maintain social distancing.

Vos and Fitzgerald assured everyone that it was going to be safe to vote, and then Vos appeared at his polling place all garbed up in medical gear, saying infamously that it was "incredibly safe."

Vos and Fitzgerald refused to change the date of the April election because they saw a political advantage in suppressing the vote, especially in a Democratic stronghold like Milwaukee, believing it would help conservative justice Daniel Kelly beat liberal judge Jill Karofksy in the Wisconsin Supreme Court race. Turns out he lost anyway.

For Vos and Fitzgerald, politics is just a game. On April 7, 2020, they turned it into a potentially lethal one.

As Debra Cronmiller, executive director of the League of Women Voters of Wisconsin, noted in a statement on its website, the actions of state officials "effectively disenfranchised hundreds of thousands of voters, most acutely people of color, people with disabilities, elderly people, students, and people who are transient." She concluded: "This is not how democracy is supposed to work. . . . It was either show up and risk your health or lose your right to vote. That is the burden that our state's leaders put on us as constituents. This is unconscionable—a violation of voters' constitutional rights and the simple humanity that binds us all."

After this debacle, which made Wisconsin (and especially Vos) a national laughingstock, a large coalition of progressive nonprofits in Wisconsin, including the Wisconsin Democracy Campaign, sent out an open letter urging the following reforms:

- Mail a ballot to all registered voters, automatically before each election, ideally 30 days before the election date. Voters should not be required to have a witness or provide proof of an ID to request or return their ballot.
- Allow voters to return ballots multiple ways: through the mail, in secure drop boxes, and at polling locations on the day of the election.
- Every municipality should have a minimum number of polling locations within their community based on the size of the population, located in areas that can serve all populations in the municipality and allow voters to register and vote quickly and efficiently if they choose to vote in person on election day.
- Every municipality should offer in-person access to early voting and voter registration in a way that proves to be safe and secure, as well as ballot drop boxes for several weeks before Election Day.
- Voter registration should be as easy as possible through automatic voter registration in schools or at the DMV. Voters should still be able to register in person on Election Day and during early voting periods.
- The Wisconsin Elections Commission should fund public education efforts to ensure that all citizens are aware of how our voting process works and how they can participate.
- Citizens for whom English is a second language should have access to language assistance for voting. This should include access to ballots and elections materials in multiple languages, in addition to English and Spanish.

The Wisconsin Elections Commission actually did accept a few of these recommendations. It did fund public education efforts, and it did send letters to 2.7 million Wisconsinites, advising them on how to request an absentee ballot. And many clerks' offices did set up secure lock boxes for early voting.

But the Republicans continued to push their voter suppression tactics. The Republican National Committee, the Republican Party of Wisconsin, and state Republican lawmakers argued in court against any extensions on the deadline to register to vote and any extension on the handing in of absentee ballots.

On September 21, US district judge William Conley ruled against them. Issuing a preliminary injunction, he ordered an extension of the voter registration deadline, online and by mail, from October 14 to October 21. And he extended the deadline for clerks receiving absentee ballots from Election Day to November 9. Noting that the "unwary" voter may not have time to fill out the absentee ballot and mail it on time, in part because of postal delays, he concluded that "the risk of disenfranchisement of thousands of Wisconsin voters due to the Election Day receipt deadline outweighs any state interest during this pandemic." He wrote that the number of disenfranchised voters "could well exceed 100,000" if he did not extend this deadline.

Conley also lifted the arbitrary requirement that poll workers have to be residents of the county in which they serve. He noted that "both for the April and August 2020 elections, local municipalities struggled to recruit and retain sufficient poll workers, which resulted in some localities being severely limited in providing in-person voting opportunities."

He wrote: "At minimum, eliminating the residence requirement would provide greater flexibility across the state to meet unanticipated last-minute demands for staffing due to COVID-19 outbreaks or fear. . . . Recruitment of poll workers will present a tricky and fluid barrier for adequate in-person voting options up to and during Election Day." The poll worker residency requirement is likely to "burden" people's "right to vote," he wrote, and "this burden outweighs any state interest in maintaining the requirement."

But a three-judge panel on the Seventh Circuit Court of Appeals, in the case called *Democratic National Committee v. Bostelmann and Wisconsin State Legislature, Republican National Committee, and Republican Party of Wisconsin*, overturned Conley's order by a vote of 2–1. The dissenting judge, Ilana Rovner, who was appointed by president George H. W. Bush, issued a scorching statement. Calling the ruling "a travesty," she wrote: "The right to vote is a right of national citizenship. . . . It is essential to the vitality of our democratic republic. No citizen of Wisconsin should be forced to risk his or her life or well-being in order to exercise this invaluable right. Wholesale deference to a state legislature in this context essentially strips the right to vote of its constitutional protection."

Rovner did not mince words: "The inevitable result of the court's decision today will be that many thousands of Wisconsin citizens will lose their right to vote despite doing everything they reasonably can to exercise it," she said.

"Good luck, and G_d bless, Wisconsin," she concluded. "You are going to need it."

On October 27, the US Supreme Court affirmed that decision, slamming the door on Wisconsin voters whose absentee ballots were mailed within the legal timeframe but didn't arrive by November 3 because of postal delays.

In a snide opinion, justices Neil Gorsuch and Brett Kavanagh wrote: "It's not hard to imagine other judges accepting invitations to unfurl the precinct maps and decide whether States should add polling places, revise their hours, rearrange the voting booths within them, or maybe even supplement existing social distancing, hand washing, and ventilation protocols. The Constitution dictates a different approach to these how-much-is-enough questions. The Constitution provides that state legislatures—not federal judges, not state judges, not state governors, not other state officials—bear primary responsibility for setting election rules."

Writing for the liberals on the court, justice Elena Kagan addressed this argument head on: "If there is one area where deference to legislators should not shade into acquiescence, it is election law. For in that field politicians' incentives often conflict with voters' interests—that is, whenever suppressing votes benefits the lawmakers who make the rules."

Kagan also argued that the majority failed to take adequate consideration of the pandemic. "The Court's decision will disenfranchise large numbers of responsible voters in the midst of hazardous pandemic conditions," she wrote. "What will undermine the 'integrity' of that process is not the counting but instead the discarding of timely cast ballots that, because of pandemic conditions, arrive a bit after Election Day. [citation omitted] On the scales of both constitutional justice and electoral accuracy, protecting the right to vote in a health crisis outweighs conforming to a deadline created in safer days."

She concluded: "Because the Court refuses to reinstate the district court's injunction, Wisconsin will throw out thousands of timely requested and timely cast mail ballots."

As Jon Sherman, senior counsel at the Fair Elections Center and one of the lawyers for the plaintiffs in this case, told me: "The Supreme Court made clear that it will not protect voters from disenfranchisement by pandemic, disenfranchisement by ballot delivery failure, or for any other complex of reasons. Sadly, the Court doesn't even follow its own precedents and won't clarify the law except to repeatedly emphasize that it simply does not believe in judicial intervention in the election law context—unless of course it is to strike down a restriction on campaign finance."

The Wisconsin lawsuit was just one of more than forty that Republican officials around the country filed in the lead-up to the 2020 elections. But when all was said and done, their efforts failed, and Joe Biden won Wisconsin and other swing states and was elected president.

But that didn't stop Donald Trump and Republican-elected officials in Washington and Wisconsin from trying to invalidate the election and disenfranchise the tens of millions of voters who voted for Biden.

For months leading up to the election, Trump was crying about a "rigged" election and how fraudulent the mail-in ballots were going to be. In the days after the election, he kept right on going with the "rigged" rhetoric. Two days after the voting booths closed, he made an embarrassing public appearance at the White House. Whining that his opponents "were trying to steal the election," asserting that he would "win easily" if only legal votes were counted, and alleging that mail-in votes were "miraculously" turning up out of nowhere to give Joe Biden whatever margin he needed, Trump acted like no president before him in trying to discredit an election that everyone could see he was losing.

He kept at it for weeks, regularly taking to Twitter to denounce the "fraud" and to claim victory, even as the electoral map showed Joe Biden with 306 electoral votes. Trump then filed lawsuit after lawsuit in the swing states in a futile attempt to not face reality. His campaign even paid for a recount in Dane County and Milwaukee County.

Members of the Milwaukee Common Council took strong exception to this tactic. Chantia Lewis, Khalif J. Rainey, Mark A. Borkowski, Nicolas Kovac, Russell W. Stamper II, and Ashanti Hamilton issued a statement saying it was "a clear attempt to somehow cast doubt on the outcome of the election in Wisconsin by looking for evidence of non-existent voter fraud. ... To seek to delegitimize and disenfranchise voters after a clear and sizable election result (where you lost fair and square, Mr. President) is, in our view, purely evil." They also denounced it as discriminatory. "The recount, focused on Wisconsin's most diverse counties where by far the state's largest populations of Black and brown people reside, is not only without merit, it is RACIST and despicable!"

When the recount got underway in Milwaukee, Trump supporters were up to more mischief. According to the AP, "Election officials in Wisconsin's largest county accused observers for President Donald Trump on Saturday of seeking to obstruct a recount of the presidential results, in some instances by objecting to every ballot tabulators pulled to count."

None of this changed the outcome of the election, but history will note the Republican officials, nationally and in Wisconsin, who aided and abetted him in this treachery. Asked about the transition to a Biden administration, secretary of state Mike Pompeo said there would be a "smooth transition to a second Trump term." Senator Lindsey Graham of South Carolina supported Trump's intransigence and even tried to strong-arm officials in Arizona, Georgia, and Nevada. Graham also echoed Trump and Weyrich a few days after the election when he said: "If we don't do something about voting by mail, we are going to lose the ability to elect a Republican in this country." Republican majority leader Mitch McConnell played along with Trump's fantasies until the Electoral College had voted, as did senator Ted Cruz of Texas, as did almost all Republicans in Congress. Senator Mike Lee of Utah was one of the most blunt: "Democracy isn't the objective," he tweeted. "Liberty, peace, and prosperity are. ... Rank democracy can thwart that." Representative Louie Gohmert of Texas was one of the most incendiary. Speaking to the Million MAGA March ten days after the election, he called for a "revolution." He said, "This was a cheated election and we can't let it stand," adding that it would take only about 30 percent of the population to succeed if all the zealous Trump supporters rose up. And former national security advisor Michael Flynn, after being pardoned by Trump, urged him to declare martial law.

In Wisconsin, we had our own would-be coup enablers. Senator Ron Johnson, who has been rehearsing for years to be top Trump suck-up, was asked, days after the election had been called, whether he had congratulated Biden yet. Johnson's response: "No. There's nothing to congratulate him about."

Then there was Speaker Vos, who has empowered a committee to "immediately review how the election was administered." Mentioning "concerns surfacing about mail-in ballot dumps and voter fraud," he called into question "whether the vote was fair and legitimate."

On that committee sits Joe Sanfelippo, of New Berlin, who went much further, saying the results of the election should actually be nullified if irregularities were found. "You either have to toss this election out and have a whole new election, or we have our delegates to the Electoral College vote for the person they think legitimately should have won," Sanfelippo told WISN-TV.

Toss out the election?!?

A conservative group actually asked the Wisconsin Supreme Court to do just that and disenfranchise the 3.24 million Wisconsinites who cast their ballots during the election. In *Wisconsin Voters Alliance v. Wisconsin Elections Commission*, the Wisconsin Supreme Court turned that down, by a 4–3 vote, with Brian Hagedorn, a swing-vote conservative justice, writing for the majority. He called the request to have the court invalidate the November election "unprecedented in American history" and "the most dramatic invocation of judicial power I have ever seen."

He added: "Judicial acquiescence to such entreaties built on so flimsy a foundation would do indelible damage to every future election. Once the door is opened to judicial invalidation of presidential election results, it will be awfully hard to close that door again. This is a dangerous path we are being asked to tread. The loss of public trust in our constitutional order resulting from the exercise of this kind of judicial power would be incalculable."

And on December 1, Trump went to the Wisconsin Supreme Court in a bogus effort to try to overturn the results of the state's presidential election, which Joe Biden won by more than twenty thousand votes.

Trump asked the court to nullify Governor Evers's certification of the results and tried to cast doubt on who the Wisconsin electors to the Electoral College should be. Not citing any incidence of fraud, the Trump lawsuit instead went after whole categories of ballots and sought to "exclude as defective . . . In-Person Absentee Ballots without an associated written application, Incomplete and Altered Certification Absentee Ballots, Indefinitely Confined Absentee Ballots, . . . and 'Democracy in the Park' Absentee Ballots."

In a legal brief, Evers's lawyer Jeffrey Mandell submitted a blistering rebuttal.

"President Trump's Petition seeks nothing less than to overturn the will of nearly 3.3 million Wisconsin voters," Mandell wrote. "It is a shocking and outrageous assault on our democracy." He added that Trump's "intent is not to fairly determine who Wisconsinites voted for to lead our country. He is simply trying to seize Wisconsin's electoral votes, even though he lost the statewide election."

Mandell argued convincingly that a ruling in favor of Trump would violate the due process guarantees in the US Constitution because it "would constitute a mass deprivation of Wisconsinites' constitutional right to vote." He added: "The due process deprivation would be particularly egregious here, where President Trump seeks to nullify votes that were lawfully cast under the rules in place at the time they voted."

He also argued that it would violate the equal protection clause of the Fourteenth Amendment because Trump urged that ballots be discarded from only Dane and Milwaukee Counties. "Granting such relief, jerry-rigged to benefit President Trump's interests, would clearly violate equal protection by treating voters in those two counties differently—less favorably—than similarly situated voters in all of Wisconsin's other counties," Mandell wrote. He also contended that Trump's claims, even if true, would amount to no more than "immaterial errors or omissions," which would not be sufficient under federal law to throw out the ballots.

Mandell then proceeded to poke big holes in Trump's assertions of fact.

For instance, Trump's lawsuit claimed that "28,395 absentee ballots were counted that were improperly cast by individuals claiming Indefinite Confinement status even as there was 'reliable information' that the elector no longer qualifies for this service." Mandell pointed out that "state law entrusts individual voters to determine whether they qualify to avail themselves of" this designation "and does not require that municipal clerks independently verify a voter's indefinitely confined status."

State law requires a clerk to remove a voter from the indefinitely confined list only "upon receipt of reliable information that [a voter] no longer qualifies for the service." Mandell noted: "President Trump fails to give even one example of a municipal clerk receiving 'reliable information' and failing to remove a voter from the list. Yet President Trump seeks to strike every vote cast by a voter indefinitely confined."

The Trump campaign lost in circuit court and appealed to the Wisconsin Supreme Court. On December 14, 2020, in *Donald J. Trump, et al v. Joseph R.*

Biden, et al, the court ruled against Trump on a 4–3 vote. Hagedorn once again wrote the majority decision. "The Campaign's request to strike indefinitely confined voters in Dane and Milwaukee Counties as a class without regard to whether any individual voter was in fact indefinitely confined has no basis in reason or law; it is wholly without merit." The other challenges, Hagedorn wrote, were filed too late: "The Campaign's delay in raising these issues was unreasonable in the extreme, and the resulting prejudice to the election officials, other candidates, voters of the affected counties, and to voters statewide, is obvious and immense. . . . The Campaign is not entitled to the relief it seeks."

That same week, Trump's lawyers filed another lawsuit, this time in federal court, urging that the results of the presidential election be invalidated. It requested the federal court to "immediately remand this matter to the Wisconsin Legislature to review . . . and determine the appropriate remedy for the constitutional violation(s) established, including any impact upon the allocation of Presidential electors for the State of Wisconsin." This lawsuit also failed, as did a lawsuit from the Texas attorney general and other attorneys general asking the US Supreme Court to invalidate the voting in Wisconsin and other swing states.

Meanwhile, the investigation that Vos ordered led to a joint legislative committee hearing on December 11. The day before that hearing, I wrote a letter to the chairs, assembly representative Ron Tusler and senator Kathy Bernier.

"Please do not bow to political pressure ginned up by a President who has neither the dignity to concede when he has lost nor the decency to uphold the norms of our treasured democracy," I urged. "Please use the power and authority you have to speak the truth, to point out the irrational, to calm the frenzied, and above all, to defend democracy itself."

Instead, the hearing they presided over on December 11 was a partisan circus. Their lead-off witness was right-wing radio's Dan O'Donnell, who rashly spoke of knowing that dead people had voted. Other "witnesses" made similarly outrageous claims. The chairs refused to require that witnesses take an oath to tell the truth, even though Democrats proposed this and cited the statutory backing for it. Nor did the chairs bother to invite the staff director of the Wisconsin Elections Board or any of the Democratic members of that board. Instead, they were content to let the reckless accusations fly, no matter the damage they were doing.

That's how far the madness went in 2020, when our entire system of democracy faced an unprecedented strain from Trump and his antidemocratic accomplices. Fortunately, the system survived, but the assault on our democracy revealed how shaky our much-ballyhooed system of checks and balances actually is.

SOLUTIONS

To make voting easier in Wisconsin, we need to repeal the voter ID law, first and foremost.

Then we need to offer mail-in voting even when there isn't a pandemic. Mail-in voting is already the practice in Colorado, Hawaii, Oregon, Utah, and Washington. There is no reason it can't be the practice in Wisconsin as well. What's more, our members of the armed services and other citizens stationed overseas have been voting by mail for a long time. These voters "can register to vote and request an absentee ballot at the same time, with one easy form," wrote reporter Alex Seitz-Wald of NBC.com on April 19, 2020. "They can receive their blank ballot by mail, fax, or email. And they will automatically be sent an absentee ballot for every election in the upcoming year, instead of having to request one each time. There's even an emergency backup ballot if the absentee ballot doesn't arrive in time. It's a blank, universal write-in ballot that can be used for any election in any state. It can be printed out and returned by mail, postage paid."

Another fundamental solution is Automatic Voter Registration, which eighteen states and the District of Columbia use, according to the National Conference of State Legislatures.

Automatic Voter Registration (AVR) registers you, if you're a citizen, when you get your driver's license at the DMV and, in some states, when you interact with other state agencies.

"AVR is a highly effective way to bring more people into our democracy," concludes "AVR Impact on State Voter Registration," a Brennan Center study from April 2019. "AVR markedly increases the number of voters being registered—increases in the number of registrants ranging from 9 to 94 percent."

Evers, it should be noted, proposed AVR in his budget, but the Republican leadership took that out too. The governor's proposal would have allowed for registration at the DMV and also sought to extend it to citizens who give their information to the Wisconsin Department of Revenue, the

Department of Health Services, the Department of Children and Families, the Department of Workforce Development, the Department of Natural Resources, and the Department of Safety and Professional Services.

When that failed, Democratic legislators introduced a stand-alone bill to accomplish AVR and also prohibit "any person from intentionally deceiving any other person regarding the date, time, place, or manner" regarding an election. A violator could be "fined not more than $100,000 or imprisoned for not more than five years, or both." The bill would also increase the fine against anyone who uses force or threatens to use force or intimidation against anyone trying to vote. The fine would jump from "not more than $10,000" to "not more than $100,000." And the bill would create a Voter Bill of Rights to be displayed at every polling place.

Our neighboring states of Illinois and Michigan have it. There's no good reason we can't have it too—and other reforms to end voter suppression and make voting easier.

Let's be clear: Voter suppression is un-democratic small *d*, and un-American, capital *A*. Every citizen has the right to vote. That right shouldn't be impeded.

The art of politics should consist of two things: getting your people out, and convincing a fraction of those who don't already agree with you that your view of what is good and right and moral and American is the best way to go.

It shouldn't be about getting fewer people to vote. It shouldn't be about forcing voters who disagree with you to run an obstacle course on the way to the voting booth.

COUNTERARGUMENTS AND COMPLEXITIES
Mail-In Voting Increases the Chances of Voter Fraud

This was the claim that Donald Trump kept repeating, ad nauseam. Asked about voting by mail during the Wisconsin election on April 7, 2020, in the midst of the coronavirus pandemic, Trump said: "Mail ballots are a very dangerous thing for this country, because they're cheaters. They go and collect them. They're fraudulent in many cases. . . . Mail ballots—they cheat. OK? People cheat. There's a lot of dishonesty going along with mail-in voting."

Leaving aside that Trump himself has voted by mail, the evidence of mail-in voter fraud is extremely negligible. As NBC News reported, "Richard Hasen, an election law expert and a professor at the University of California,

Irvine, pointed to an exhaustive News21 review of voter fraud between 2000 and 2012, which found just 491 incidents of alleged absentee voter fraud among more than a decade of elections and 146 million registered voters."

Republicans Would Never Win with Mail-In Ballots

On this one, Trump let the cat out of the bag. At that same press conference on April 7, 2020, he said if there was ever national mail-in voting, the "levels of voting" would be so high that "you'd never have a Republican elected in this country again."

He was thereby conceding the point that Republicans want fewer citizens to vote because they know they do better with a low turnout. Here he was simply echoing on national TV the comment that Paul Weyrich made to the gathering of the religious right forty years before.

But if Republicans can't win with a large turnout, they shouldn't change the way we vote to make voting harder. They should change what they stand for to appeal to more people!

Civic Tradition Deteriorates with Early and Mail-In Voting

The National Conference of State Legislators says that one possible disadvantage of early and mail-in voting is the loss of "the civic experience of voting with neighbors at a local school, church, or other polling place."

There is something to be said for this argument. For most of my adult life, I've enjoyed the civic experience of voting with my fellow citizens on Election Day. There are far too few civic events where we come together as one, so I get it. But this loss has to be balanced against the gains of greater voter turnout, and on that scale, greater turnout wins.

Early Voting Is a Risk Because Situations May Change at the End

One risk of early voting is that people are casting their ballots before all the evidence is in. For instance, something could come out about a candidate in the last week of a campaign that might change the minds of people who have already voted. Or a candidate might make a horrible blunder in the last few days on the trail or in a final debate. Or, in a primary, your candidate may already have dropped out. This argument arose during the 2020 Democratic primaries when a lot of the candidates cleared the field for Joe Biden even after many people had already sent in their ballots. Many people ended up voting for candidates who were no longer in the race, so their votes were wasted.

You can envision other situations where this might be an even bigger problem. What if one of the leading candidates drops dead before the date of the primary but after a lot of the early votes have been cast? Again, a lot of votes would be wasted, and the ability to get your voice heard at the ballot box, at a consequential moment, would be lost.

So, yes, this is a risk. But again, I don't believe it outweighs the benefits of high voter turnout.

chapter 4

Reenfranchise Former Prisoners

Carl Fields grew up in Racine. He was incarcerated for sixteen years after he exchanged gunfire with the police. Fortunately, no one was injured. Fields was released in 2016, but he won't be able to vote for another sixteen years.

"I get off paper in 2033," he told me, referring to the extended supervision that he's on. Wisconsin, unlike many states, won't let prisoners vote when they get out of prison but only when they're off supervision, probation, and parole.

"It's frustrating, it's disheartening," says Fields. "I'm being told that I'm a citizen again and that I should interact with the community, but then they want me to do everything but be a citizen."

Fields, who is the Kenosha-Racine organizer for Ex-incarcerated People Organizing (EXPO), believes that former prisoners ought to be full citizens. "Once you get home and you're in the community and you're paying taxes and participating, you should have a say in how your taxes are spent. You should have a say in your schools and who is picking up your garbage. Now I can't really be a part of the community; I can only look the part."

Fields says this deprives him of a basic American right: "No taxation without representation," he argues. "Having a vote means having a say. Having a say means having control over your own life. Having control of your life is a kind of empowerment that can change the system from the inside out."

In Wisconsin in 2020, about forty-five thousand formerly incarcerated people like Fields were being denied their right to vote. They are "highly skewed toward African American folks and poor people, and that skews the electorate," says David Liners, the executive director of WISDOM, a Wisconsin network of faith-based organizations that works on prison issues.

In its report "Unlock the Vote Wisconsin!" the ACLU of Wisconsin noted, "Though African-Americans comprise only 5 percent of the voting age population, they make up 39 percent of the disfranchised population. One in 9 African-American voters is disfranchised in Wisconsin, compared to 1 in 50 of all Wisconsin voters."

Policies vary from state to state on the right of prisoners or ex-prisoners to vote. Few people know that in two states, people behind bars actually have the right to vote. The answer to this little pop quiz is Maine and Vermont.

In many states, you can vote as soon as you leave prison. That's the case in our neighboring states of Illinois and Michigan, as well as Colorado, the District of Columbia, Hawaii, Indiana, Maryland, Massachusetts, Montana, Nevada, New Hampshire, North Dakota, Ohio, Oregon, Pennsylvania, Rhode Island, and Utah. In two states, Iowa and Kentucky, if you commit a felony, you can never vote again, no matter how long you've been out of prison and off paper. At least that was the case until December 2019, when Kentucky governor Andy Beshear signed an executive order to restore voting rights for more than 140,000 nonviolent offenders who have completed their sentences.

Florida also used to disenfranchise felons for life until the citizenry, in November 2018, after an amazing grassroots campaign, passed a referendum to reenfranchise former felons. Republicans in the legislature then passed a bill to deprive them of the vote if they had any unpaid court fees or fines. In the case *Kelvin Leon Jones, et al v. Ron DeSantis, et al*, US district judge Robert Hinkle ruled that "Florida cannot deny restoration of a felon's right to vote solely because the felon does not have the financial resources necessary to pay restitution." But the US Court of Appeals for the Eleventh Circuit overturned that decision in a 6–4 ruling. Desmond Meade, executive director of the Florida Rights Restoration Coalition, called this a "severe blow to democracy."

In California, Connecticut, and New York, former felons can vote once they've completed parole. The remainder of the states, like Wisconsin, don't allow former felons to vote unless they are off some combination of parole, probation, and postsentencing supervision.

Fields, who is Black, traces this disenfranchisement to the very roots of racism in the United States. "It ties back to the whole three-fifths rule," he says, citing the Constitution's dehumanization of slaves. "We've never gotten away from that system."

Fields is on to something. Using prison sentences to disenfranchise Black people was an explicit strategy of the Jim Crow South. After Reconstruction, many southern states rewrote their constitutions with the express purpose of kicking Black people off the rolls.

In Alabama, for instance, the president of the state's 1901 constitutional convention, John Knox, said the goal of the convention was "to establish white supremacy in this State. . . . We must establish it by law—not by force or fraud." This was necessary, he said, to counter "the menace of Negro domination."

So the 1901 Alabama Constitution said:

> The following persons shall be disqualified both from registering, and from voting, namely:
>
> All idiots and insane persons; those who shall by reason of conviction of crime be disqualified from voting at the time of the ratification of this Constitution; those who shall be convicted of treason, murder, arson, embezzlement, malfeasance in office, larceny, receiving stolen property, obtaining property or money under false pretenses, perjury, subornation of perjury, robbery, assault with intent to rob, burglary, forgery, bribery, assault and battery on the wife, bigamy, living in adultery, sodomy, incest, rape, miscegenation, crime against nature, or any crime punishable by imprisonment in the penitentiary, or of any infamous crime or crime involving moral turpitude.

Or take Virginia. State representative Carter Glass introduced a bill around the same time that he said would "eliminate the darkey as a political factor . . . in less than five years." He said his goal was "to discriminate to the very extremity . . . with a view to the elimination of every negro voter who can be gotten rid of."

In Wisconsin, our state constitution, which was written in 1848, gave the legislature the authority to restrict felons' right to vote. In 1947, according to the ACLU of Wisconsin, this authority was clarified to mean that felons could not vote until completion of their entire sentence.

In its implementation, the disenfranchisement of formerly incarcerated felons has had a ripple effect throughout communities of color, and it has reduced their political power across the board.

"Felony disfranchisement laws bar individuals from voting not only in presidential elections but also in local elections for city council, school board, and other positions," the ACLU of Wisconsin noted in its report. "As such, many parents are prevented from having a say in important issues affecting their families. In hypersegregated communities like Milwaukee where disfranchisement rates are particularly high, this can be devastating to the entire community."

Jerome Dillard is the state director of EXPO. A former prisoner himself, Dillard stresses the importance of restoring former prisoners' voting rights. "It's the right thing to do," he says. "I know so many individuals who are working really hard in this community. They're paying their taxes. But still they can't vote, and they have no say in what services they get, in who represents their community, and who's on the school board." Dillard, who is Black, says, "This disenfranchisement is a throwback to Jim Crow."

Liners of WISDOM says that not letting former prisoners vote is counterproductive. "Not that voting is a magic bullet to avoid recidivism, but if people feel they have a stake in what's going on, they're more likely to work within the system," he says. "If they feel completely shut out, if they feel, 'I'm not part of the democracy, I'm not part of the community, I'm a pariah, that's my role,' then we're sending a message when we do this."

Ed Wall, who was secretary of corrections under governor Scott Walker, agrees: "If we encourage former felons to become successful, find and maintain employment, pay taxes, and contribute to society, then why would we stop them from voting? It seems to me that if a person is getting their life turned around, we should embrace that mindset."

SOLUTIONS

In the Wisconsin legislature, senator Lena Taylor and representative David Crowley (now Milwaukee county executive) have been strong advocates for the reenfranchisement of former felons and have introduced bills to make this happen.

"It's so unfair that people are being denied the right to vote even after they've been released," says Taylor. "People are denied a voice, denied an opportunity to weigh in on anything." Taylor, who believes that people who are incarcerated should be allowed to vote while behind bars, understands that politically it will be a battle to get back even former prisoners' right to vote.

"Legislators are going to have to see beyond themselves and see beyond whatever underlying beliefs that they have about people who are incarcerated," says Taylor.

Crowley agrees: "It's going to be an uphill struggle but we have to continue to move forward," he told me. "At the end of the day, we talk about giving folks second chances. It's important after they've paid their debt to society. They deserve a second chance."

COUNTERARGUMENTS AND COMPLEXITIES

Former Prisoners Don't Deserve It

One argument against reenfranchising former prisoners is symbolic or moralistic: by committing a felony, a serious crime against society, the individual has forfeited his or her right to participate fully in society. This concept, which derives from the doctrine of "civic death" in ancient Greece and Rome and in Anglo-Saxon law, may have some emotional tug to it. But the idea that former prisoners don't deserve to participate fully in our society is belied by the law in forty-eight of the fifty states, which allow former prisoners, at some point, to vote again. So the emotional tug wears off after one has served his or her time, or finished with probation, parole, and extended supervision. Almost all states have come to realize that "civic death" is too harsh a sentence.

Chief justice Earl Warren came to the same conclusion when he wrote, in the 1958 case *Trop v. Dulles*: "Citizenship is not a right that expires upon misbehavior."

Variants of the moralistic argument include the claim that forbidding former prisoners from voting promotes respect for the rule of law. This is a hard-to-quantify and implausible claim. It seems unlikely that the general public has an increased respect for the rule of law because many former prisoners can't vote; most people are unaware of—or unclear on—whether former prisoners can vote or not. And as for the former prisoners themselves, it's doubtful that the added punishment of not being able to vote makes them more respectful of the law than the punishment of serving many years behind bars.

Those Who Commit the Most Heinous Crimes Don't Deserve It

When Floridians voted overwhelmingly in 2018 to reenfranchise former felons, they exempted murderers and rapists. Again, you can feel the emotional tug and detect the political motive as well: it would have been a harder sell at the ballot box if opponents were running lurid commercials about the most horrible murderers and rapists who were about to get their voting rights back.

But neither the emotional tug nor the political incentive is persuasive. The principle is the same, whether the crime is armed robbery, for instance, or murder or rape: once you've served your debt to society, you should get your rights back. Former felons in Florida who were convicted of rape or murder may have a Fourteenth Amendment case to bring here.

As Justice Thurgood Marshall wrote in his dissent in *Richardson v. Ramirez* (1974), criminal disenfranchisement "must be measured against the requirements of the Equal Protection Clause of Section One of the Fourteenth Amendment."

What's more, because crimes of murder and rape are not aimed at our political system itself, stripping these individuals of the suffrage makes less sense than, say, doing so to those who committed crimes like political bribery or voter fraud, or attacks and threats against elected officials—crimes that are directly related to, and undermine, our democratic system. I'm not in favor of that, by the way, but at least I can understand the argument.

Former Prisoners Will Vote to Subvert Our Justice System

US appellate judge Henry Friendly, in *Green v. Board of Elections* (1967), made probably the most famous articulation of this argument when he wrote:

> It can scarcely be deemed unreasonable for a state to decide that perpetrators of serious crimes shall not take part in electing the legislators who make the laws, the executives who enforce these, the prosecutors who must try them for further violations, or the judges who are to consider their cases. This is especially so when account is taken of the heavy incidence of recidivism and the prevalence of organized crime.... A contention that the Equal Protection Clause requires New York to allow convicted Mafiosi to vote for district attorneys or judges would not only be without merit but as obviously so as anything that might be.

But the flaw in Judge Friendly's argument is that the Mob doesn't have enough people to elect a judge or a district attorney. That's why the Mob traditionally tried more direct routes, like buying off judges and DAs, or threatening them.

A related argument is that a bunch of former prisoners will band together and advocate for more leniency within the criminal justice system. But that should be their right! And they won't succeed, just like other advocates, unless they can convince a majority of the people in their state about the validity of their positions.

Justice Marshall, again in his *Richardson* dissent, addressed the claim that it's important "to keep former felons from voting because their likely voting pattern might be subversive to the interests of an orderly society."

As Marshall wrote: "The ballot is the democratic system's coin of the realm. To condition its exercise on support of the established order is to debase that currency beyond recognition."

chapter 5

End Prison Gerrymandering

If you're a Black man from Milwaukee who was convicted of a felony on April 2, 2020, and you were sent to prison in Waupun for two years, the 2020 census counts you as living not in Milwaukee but in Waupun. And it counts you as living in Waupun until the next census, in 2030, even if you return to your home in Milwaukee, zip code 53206, after serving your two years.

In Waupun, you're being "represented" in the Wisconsin legislature by two conservative white Republicans, representative Michael Schraa and senator Dan Feyen, instead of by the Black Democrats from your district, representative David Bowen and senator Lena Taylor.

On top of that, the census helps determine the flow of federal dollars to local districts, per capita. Wisconsin has one of the nation's highest rates of Black incarceration, so predominantly white Waupun is getting more money, and Milwaukee, which is about 40 percent Black, is getting less.

This is what's called "prison gerrymandering": the racially distorted representation and the racially distorted distribution of resources, based on the way the census counts prisoners.

The district that Bowen and Taylor represent has the highest incarceration rate in the state. Many of their former constituents are sent off to Waupun or other prisons around the state that are in rural, white areas.

"Our communities are losing resources" because of prison gerrymandering, Taylor says. "Those dollars are lost. They're going to communities that the prisoners have never lived in. I'd like to see those dollars go to communities that need the services."

Jerome Dillard of EXPO points out that rural white communities are getting extra resources because they have a high prison population. "Dodge

County is huge when it comes to prison gerrymandering," he says, rattling off the prisons there: Waupun, Fox Lake, Dodge, and Burke. It's especially galling to Dillard that prisoners are counted as living there even after they're out. "If you leave Dodge [Correctional Facility] in 2021, they get money for you for the next nine years. You're a ghost. You don't live there anymore. You're not counted in the community you came from and go back to—a community that really needs those resources."

When the NPR podcast *Code Switch* looked at prison gerrymandering in Wisconsin, on October 2, 2019, it focused on how the practice denies persons who are incarcerated of adequate representation. Reporter Hansi Lo Wang visited the city of Waupun, where prisoners make up more than a quarter of the population. He interviewed a prisoner named Kenneth McGowan and asked him if he considered himself a resident of Waupun.

"No, not at all," McGowan said, telling Wang that he's from Milwaukee and his "mother, father, three sisters, nieces, and nephews" still live there.

The local alderperson who supposedly "represents" the people in the prison is Peter Kaczmarski. Prisoners make up about 76 percent of his district, Wang reported. Wang asked McGowan if he had ever heard of Kaczmarski.

"Not at all," said McGowan. "Not until you came."

McGowan could use some decent local representation. "The drinking water in prison is horrible," he said. "When you push the button, sometimes it comes out brown."

Wang talked to Kaczmarski, who told him he has "never visited Waupun Correctional Institution" and acknowledged that "it's right down the street from my home." He added: "You almost have to think for them because you don't, perhaps, have that day-to-day interaction."

Waupun is but one example. According to the Prison Policy Initiative, a national nonprofit based in Massachusetts, prison gerrymandering occurs in other places in Wisconsin. It notes these rates of incarceration: 80 percent of a district in Juneau County, 62 percent of two districts in Adams County, and 51 percent of a district in Jackson County.

SOLUTIONS

Prison gerrymandering is part of the representational crisis we're facing in Wisconsin and around the country. Some other states are doing something about it. In 2020, Colorado, Nevada, New Jersey, Virginia, and Washington all banned it, joining California, Maryland, and New York among the states that have ended this practice.

In 2018, the NAACP in Connecticut filed a pathbreaking federal lawsuit, *NAACP Connecticut, et al v. Denise Merrill, et al*, challenging that state's prison gerrymandering. It "violates the 'one person, one vote' principle of the Fourteenth Amendment to the United States Constitution," the lawsuit says. "It impermissibly inflates the voting strength of predominantly white voters residing in certain Connecticut House and Senate Districts. . . . By counting prisoners in the districts where they are imprisoned instead of their pre-incarceration residences, prison gerrymandering dilutes the votes of residents in their home communities, who are disproportionately African-American and Latino."

It further notes: "Persons incarcerated in districts far from their home communities have no meaningful connection to the towns in which they are incarcerated. . . . Local legislators do not visit prisoners incarcerated in their districts. Consequently, the districts' representatives do not, in practice, represent these incarcerated persons or perform legislative services for them."

In February 2019, a district court judge refused to dismiss this lawsuit. And in September 2019, an appellate panel upheld that ruling and sent the case back to district court, saying that claims by the NAACP were "neither frivolous nor insubstantial."

Here in Wisconsin, in the 2018–19 legislative session, Taylor and Crowley introduced a bill that would ban prison gerrymandering. It would count prisoners as residing in the communities where they were living "prior to being confined."

Says Crowley, who is now Milwaukee county executive: "Ending prison gerrymandering is one of the most fundamental things we can do to give people one person, one vote."

COUNTERARGUMENTS AND COMPLEXITIES
Local Communities Deserve the Extra Resources

When Colorado was debating whether to ban prison gerrymandering, which it did in March 2020, Republican legislators who opposed it, and who had prisons in their district, claimed that it would be unfair to the communities that house the prisons.

"When you have a prison in the community, it affects the entire community," said state senator Jerry Sonnenberg, who has four prisons in his district. "To have them counted somewhere else, I think, will do an injustice to the communities that actually holds those prisons."

It's an amorphous argument. Of course, having a prison "affects the entire community." But how? It brings jobs, for one thing, and that's not a negative. Prisons have often been sold as a rural development strategy for poor towns, though the evidence is mixed on that front.

Some of the possible economic downsides include a small "multiplier" effect, compared to development strategies that might boost other related industries, as Tracy Huling noted in her essay "Building a Prison Economy in Rural America," in *Invisible Punishment: The Collateral Consequences of Mass Imprisonment.*

Huling also noted that "the impact of prisons on housing can also cause economic hardships for the poor and elderly in rural communities. Both land and rental values generally increase when a prison siting is authorized by a governmental or corporate entity; however, land values fall once the actual (low) number of locally gained jobs, and associated homeowners, becomes clear. This has the effect of placing additional burdens on poorer members of the community, particularly renters and elderly homeowners."

She added: "The 'hidden' costs of doing prison business can be high for small communities. Local court and police systems are often the first to feel the impact. In many states county or district public defenders are responsible for defending indigent inmates charged with committing crimes (e.g., assaults on guards and other inmates) within state prisons. In low-population counties with large numbers of prisoners, the prisoner share of a defender's caseload can be quite high."

According to the Real Cost of Prisons Project, "Over the past 25 years, most prison towns have grown poorer and more desperate."

So there is some evidence that communities that house prisons do bear some extra costs. But you need to balance that claim against the claims on the other side: prisoners deserve to be counted in the communities that they come from, and those communities are being stripped of resources because prisoners aren't being counted there. On balance, those claims are much more persuasive.

What about Prisoners Who Are in for More than a Decade?

One of the strongest arguments for banning prison gerrymandering is that it counts a prisoner as living where the prison is located even if that prisoner gets out a month after the census and moves back to his or her home in another community. "About 75% of all people got out of prison within 48 months of entering," wrote UW sociology professor Pamela Oliver in a December 22, 2016, article titled "How Long Do People Stay in Prison in Wisconsin?" It's wrong and misleading to count these people as residing in the prison for ten years, which is what the census does.

But what about those who are in the same prison for more than a decade? "About 12% are still in prison after 14 years (168 months); these are usually people with long sentences for very serious crimes," notes Oliver.

Here the logic of counting this small minority as residents of the community where the prison is located is stronger. But what if a person who was in for ten years as of January 2020 was released on August 1, 2020, a few months after the census, and went back to his or her home community: should that person be counted as living where the prison is located?

Even with this small population of prisoners with lengthy sentences, the problems of prison gerrymandering persist.

chapter 6

Tighten Recusal Rules

It's not every day that the chief justice of the Wisconsin Supreme Court goes after me, but that's what happened on March 7, 2017. On that day, Patience Roggensack went to Marquette University Law School to give the annual Hallows Lecture. She was not in a very judicious frame of mind, however, as she lashed out at her critics. She castigated fellow justices Shirley Abrahamson and Ann Walsh Bradley. She threw a dart at former justice Janine Geske, who was in the audience and who teaches at Marquette. And she took issue with something I wrote for the Wisconsin Democracy Campaign, the organization I head.

Roggensack said she was concerned about protecting "the institutional legitimacy of our courts," arguing that "tough talk" from critics was undermining it, and she specifically mentioned the Wisconsin Democracy Campaign. I believe the tough talk from me that she didn't take a shine to was when I called the Wisconsin Supreme Court a "corrupt, rigged, and renegade court."

I had done so in an article posted on our website on December 7, 2015, where I had added, for good measure, that the high court is "an embarrassment to the state, and it's a joke on the justice system."

(Yeah, I know, I don't hold back. I let people know how I really feel.)

What had gotten my juices flowing was the court's dismissal of the case against governor Scott Walker on specious grounds. That case, known as *John Doe II*, involved the question of whether Walker was illegally coordinating with outside electioneering groups.

In its July 16, 2015, decision ordering an end to *John Doe II*, the court came up with an interpretation of the First Amendment to the US Constitution that was at odds with the US Supreme Court's view. The Wisconsin court said that the First Amendment prohibits a ban on coordination between candidates and issue advocacy groups. But four decades of the US court's decisions, dating back to *Buckley v. Valeo* in 1976 and right on through *Citizens United* of 2010, have been predicated on there being no coordination between candidates and outside groups.

In *Buckley*, the court ruled that expenditures by outside groups that are coordinated with candidates amount to campaign contributions. "The ultimate effect is the same as if the person had contributed the dollar amount to the candidate and the candidate had then used the contribution," the court ruled. Such expenditures, it said, should be "treated as contributions rather than expenditures."

Only the lack of coordination reduces the risk of corruption, the court stressed in *Buckley*. "The absence of prearrangement and coordination of an expenditure with the candidate or his agent . . . alleviates the danger that expenditures will be given as a quid pro quo for improper commitments from the candidates."

Even in its infamous *Citizens United* decision, which allowed independent groups to spend unlimited amounts of money, the US Supreme Court stressed that such groups had to be independent; they couldn't coordinate with their favored candidates: "By definition, an independent expenditure is political speech presented to the electorate that is not coordinated with a candidate."

But the so-called conservatives on the Wisconsin Supreme Court simply chose to ignore these precedents and rule whatever way they wanted.

At least two of them shouldn't even have been sitting on the case. They should have recused themselves. (To "recuse oneself" means to get off a case because of a conflict of interest or the appearance of a conflict of interest.) Justices David Prosser and Michael Gableman were asked by the special prosecutor, Francis Schmitz, to recuse themselves since he was investigating Wisconsin Manufacturers & Commerce and Wisconsin Club for Growth, which had spent huge amounts on their behalf ($1.6 million to help elect Prosser and $2.26 million to help elect Gableman. They also spent $850,000 to help elect Roggensack).

But neither Gableman nor Prosser recused himself, despite clear guidance from the US Supreme Court.

In *Williams-Yulee v. Florida Bar* (2015), which was decided just two and a half months before the Wisconsin Supreme Court deep-sixed the *John Doe II* case, the US Supreme Court ruled: "Even if judges were able to refrain from favoring donors, the mere possibility that judges' decisions may be motivated by the desire to repay campaign contributions is likely to undermine the public's confidence in the judiciary."

And in *Caperton v. Massey Coal* (2009), the US Supreme Court ruled that a judge or justice needs to recuse himself or herself when the degree of campaign spending is such that "the probability of actual bias on the part of the judge or decision maker is too high to be constitutionally tolerable." The *Caperton* case is especially instructive. Plaintiff Hugh Caperton had sued the Massey Coal company, and a trial court in West Virginia had found Massey Coal liable for $50 million in damages. Massey Coal appealed to the West Virginia Supreme Court, and Massey's CEO, Donald Blankenship, donated $3 million to the supreme ourt candidacy of Brent Benjamin, who ended up winning. Benjamin then gave the decisive vote, in a 3–2 decision, throwing out the lower court's verdict against the company.

Caperton appealed to the US Supreme Court, claiming that he didn't get a fair trial because of Blankenship's huge donation to Benjamin. The court agreed, ruling that letting Benjamin sit on this case violated Caperton's due process rights.

Its decision invited states to "adopt recusal standards more rigorous than due process requires." Wisconsin has not taken up that invitation. Quite the contrary. In fact, one year after the *Massey* decision, it did the reverse.

Asked by the League of Women Voters of Wisconsin to tighten its recusal rules, the Wisconsin Supreme Court went a different route and sided with Wisconsin Manufacturers & Commerce and the Wisconsin Realtors Association. Those two groups actually helped draft the new rule that the court adopted, which states, in part: "A judge shall not be required to recuse himself or herself in a proceeding based solely on any endorsement or the judge's campaign committee's receipt of a lawful campaign contribution, including a campaign contribution from an individual or entity involved in the proceeding."

They left it totally up to the judge or justice!

Almost two years after the *John Doe II* decision came down, fifty-four retired judges with a combined service of more than 1,100 years on the Wisconsin bench petitioned the court to tighten its recusal rules. These judges have had extremely distinguished careers. The list includes two former justices of the Wisconsin Supreme Court, eleven chief judges, several judges who've been named "judge of the year" by the Wisconsin Bar Association, and two judges who've received a "lifetime achievement award."

Their petition urged the court "to establish an objective standard requiring recusal or disqualification of a judge when he or she has received the benefit of campaign contributions or assistance from a party or lawyer." The petition states: "As money in elections becomes more predominant, citizens rightfully ask whether justice is for sale. The appearance of partiality that large campaign donations cause strikes at the heart of the judicial function, which depends on the public's respect for its judgments."

The petition also noted that the Center for American Progress ranked Wisconsin forty-seventh out of the fifty states in having adequate recusal rules in place. As the petition says, "Well-informed citizens would and do reasonably question a judge's ability to be impartial when that judge has received sizable assistance in his or her campaign from a party to a case or the party's attorney."

On behalf of the Wisconsin Democracy Campaign, I sent a letter to Chief Justice Roggensack on March 27, 2017 (I'm sure she was happy to hear from me) in support of this petition.

Here's some of that letter:

In 2010, the Court justified its lax recusal rule in part by noting that corruption by issue advocacy groups was unlikely since expenditures and communications by such groups "must be completely independent of the judge's campaign, as required by law, to retain their First Amendment protection." But in the Court's decision to shut down the John Doe II investigation, the Court said that the First Amendment prohibits the State of Wisconsin from banning coordination between candidates and issue advocacy groups. So now that these expenditures and communications need no longer "be completely independent of the judge's campaign," the risk of corruption rears its ugly head. Any justices on the Wisconsin Supreme Court running for re-election, or any other candidates for the bench, can now work with an issue advocacy group that is throwing mud at their opponents. Are we supposed to believe that the judge or justice can then remain impartial when deciding a case involving the very issue advocacy group that helped get that jurist elected? This is mind-boggling in its brazenness, and in the gullibility the Court imputes to the citizenry of Wisconsin.

On April 20, 2017, at an open administrative conference, the Wisconsin Supreme Court took up the petition. Justice Shirley Abrahamson, one of the two liberals on the court at that time, first moved that there be a public hearing. "I see no reason not to hold a public hearing on this," she said. "I can't remember any petition that has received this much comment."

Justice Ann Walsh Bradley, the other liberal, agreed: "The issue is so important that to shut it down without a hearing undermines the public confidence that is so important for this court. At least give people a chance to be heard. What is so threatening about that? I think a public hearing is absolutely essential in this case."

But shut it down they did, by a vote of 5–2.

Then the two liberal justices made a motion that the court should accept the petition from the fifty-four judges. Justice Annette Ziegler made a separate motion to reject the petition. She said the petition "just does not comport with the Constitution."

Justice Rebecca Bradley chimed in that it would violate her oath of office to uphold the Constitution because "the petition infringes the First Amendment rights of Wisconsinites who wish to participate in judicial elections. The people have a First Amendment right to speak out on issues." She also said that "this petition rests on a presumption that's false—that Wisconsin judges are incapable of deciding for themselves when they should recuse themselves. Every judge in Wisconsin should be offended by this. It attacks their integrity and character."

Later, Abrahamson responded in writing on the constitutional issue, citing case after case of US Supreme Court precedent requiring recusal in certain circumstances, including instances of campaign donations to judges. "These cases all state that due process requires recusal if there is an actual conflict of interest or the appearance of a conflict of interest," Abrahamson noted.

She quoted *Rippo v. Baker*, which had been decided just a few months before: "Under our precedents, the Due Process Clause may sometimes demand recusal even when a judge 'ha[s] no actual bias.' [citation omitted] Recusal is required when, objectively speaking, 'the probability of actual bias on the part of the judge or decisionmaker is too high to be constitutionally tolerable.'" [citation omitted]

Abrahamson also referred to the 2009 *Caperton* case, in which the court ruled: "The appearance of bias demeans the reputation and integrity of not just one jurist, but of the larger institution of which he or she is a part. . . . Both the appearance and reality of impartial justice are necessary to the public legitimacy of judicial pronouncements and thus to the rule of law itself."

In none of these cases did the US Supreme Court say that recusal rules infringe on anyone's First Amendment rights, though that's what the right-wing majority on the Wisconsin Supreme Court insisted upon. It maintained that the final word on recusal should be left up to each individual judge. "That's just not what the U.S. Supreme Court has been saying," Abrahamson wrote. "They say there is a due process right not only to fair adjudication but the perception and appearance of fair adjudication."

Ann Walsh Bradley noted that under the current recusal rules, "Judges' campaign committees can actively solicit litigants with cases before them." A couple of conservative justices asked her to name an instance of this. "The very idea causes you to be aghast," she said.

Seemingly frustrated by the action of the court, Ann Walsh Bradley said: "A fundamental tenet of our democracy is that judges must be perceived beyond price."

The right-wing majority, again by a vote of 5–2, dismissed the petition of the fifty-four retired judges.

A few of those judges were in the audience when the justices were considering their petition.

"I'm surprised they wouldn't even talk about why they wouldn't hold a public hearing on this," said retired judge William Foust.

"I just feel sad," said retired judge Sarah O'Brien. "The people believe that large campaign contributions can influence judges, but the justices refuse to acknowledge that. It's what we expected, but it's no less heartbreaking."

When the Wisconsin Supreme Court finally came out with its written order on June 30 denying the recusal petition, Justice Abrahamson would have none of it.

"The court order makes a feeble and somewhat misleading attempt to justify the dismissal," Abrahamson wrote, adding that the underlying "justifications proffered by the justices themselves . . . are, in my opinion, unsubstantiated and misguided." Her thirty-page dissent was joined by Ann Walsh Bradley.

In denying the petition, the three-page order said: "The petition presumes, as a categorical matter, that the judges and justices of this state are incapable of fulfilling their oaths to 'administer justice without respect to persons' and to 'faithfully and impartially discharge the duties of [their] office.' This is an entirely unwarranted presumption and we will not entertain it."

Abrahamson pointed out that the logic behind this claim would make any judicial code of conduct unnecessary: "No code of judicial conduct will ever be needed because the oath in general terms already prohibits much (if not all) the conduct specifically prohibited in the code. I conclude that a Code of Judicial Conduct that provides more specific direction for judges than does the oath serves judges and the public well."

Abrahamson also lit into Rebecca Bradley's claim that the petition insulted every judge in Wisconsin:

> Recusal standards are, in my opinion, no more of an insult to judges and justices than it is an insult to all law-abiding people to have laws governing ethics for public officials; laws governing criminal and tortious conduct; laws protecting our rivers, lakes, and streams; laws regulating the quality of dairy products; and so on and so forth. Unfortunately, judges and justices, like all people, even very good people, need guidance and make mistakes. . . .
>
> In a perfect world, we would not need a Code of Judicial Conduct, and we would not need many of the statutes that now cover six hefty volumes of the Wisconsin Statutes.

Abrahamson also made mincemeat out of the argument that a tighter recusal rule would somehow violate the First Amendment. "No one has cited any case (and I cannot find any) holding or even hinting that judicial recusal requirements violate a campaign donor's or a voter's (or anyone else's) First Amendment (or any other) rights."

When they want to, the so-called conservatives of the Wisconsin Supreme Court just make stuff up. So you can see why I said what I did about the court being "a corrupt, rigged, and renegade court."

SOLUTIONS

In the years since the petition by the retired judges, the issue of recusal has not gone away. Common Cause in Wisconsin has held several public events on recusal and has produced some videos online about the urgent need for it.

Representative Gary Hebl has introduced bills to tighten Wisconsin's judicial recusal rules. One of the measures would require recusal in a civil or criminal case if a party in the case contributed $1,000 or more to the judge's campaign in the previous four years. The bill would also require recusal if a party spent $1,000 or more on outside electioneering activities that spoke highly of the judge or attacked the judge's opponent.

Another Hebl proposal would require a party in a case who contributes to a judge's campaign committee to at least notify the other parties in the case about the contribution within five days.

Check this out! This is how lax our recusal laws stand right now: you can be arguing a case before an appellate judge, and you can write that judge a $5,000 check while the judge is hearing your case, and neither you nor the judge has to tell the other party about it. If that's not an open invitation to legalized judicial bribery, I don't know what is.

I was at the hearing on Hebl's bills, and I remember Republican representative Samantha Kerkman's indignation that any judge would be corrupted like this. She, too, claimed that Hebl had just insulted every judge in the state of Wisconsin. And she insisted that donors were not contributing directly to any judges but to their campaign committees.

As if there's any difference!

If someone gives a judge's campaign committee $5,000, you can bet the judge will find out about it real soon. Candidates know who their big donors are.

Who are you kidding, Kerkman?

For a decade now, Wisconsinites have been fed a steady diet of sophistry from so-called conservatives on the Wisconsin Supreme Court and by Republican legislators, claiming that we don't need strict rules on judicial recusal.

But we do.

And we need them now.

COUNTERARGUMENTS AND COMPLEXITIES
How Tightly to Draw the Line?

The fifty-four retired judges who petitioned the Wisconsin Supreme Court in 2017 for a tightening of the recusal rules drew the lines clearly and tightly. They said that if a party to a case, or the lawyer for that party, contributes the following amounts to the judge presiding over the case, then that judge has to recuse himself or herself:

- If it's a supreme court justice, the amount is $10,000.
- If it's judge on the court of appeals, it's $2,500.

- If it's a circuit court judge, it's $1,000.
- And if it's a municipal court judge, it's $500.

These amounts are equal to 50 percent of what an individual can contribute to a judge's campaign.

Interestingly, the retired judges made no distinction between direct contributions to the judge's campaign committee, independent expenditures, or contributions to a group doing independent expenditures "with the intention or reasonable expectation" that this group would use the money to influence the judge's election. All of these would constitute campaign contributions, they said.

They also said that contributions from immediate family members of a party to a case count toward these limits.

And if a corporation has been making the independent expenditures, the contributions from the CEO, executive director, managing partner, members of the board of directors, or anyone who owns at least 10 percent of the company's stock also count toward these limits.

These limits seem awfully high to me. I mean, if I gave a supreme court justice $5,000 or an appellate court judge $2,000 and they both win, and I'm in their court, I'm really in their court! Not many donors give at that level, so you can bet they would have an incentive to look more kindly upon me than my adversary.

If I were drawing the lines for recusal, I would draw them even tighter than the retired judges did. But the fact that the conservatives on the Wisconsin Supreme Court disregard even the judges' lines tells you how far we have to go to get to reasonable rules in Wisconsin that would guarantee due process—and rescind any invitation to legalized judicial bribery.

Who Would Referee?

This is always a question. But the proposal by the retired judges addressed this in a thoughtful way. It said that if a lower-court judge who is challenged to recuse himself or herself refuses to do so, the chief judge of the municipal or circuit court would decide. If the judge is on the appellate court, a randomly selected Wisconsin Supreme Court justice would decide it. If it's a supreme court justice, a panel of three randomly selected appellate court justices would decide. I don't see anything wrong with this idea. I would also be in favor of a citizens' commission, set up by the Wisconsin Supreme Court, to weigh these matters, as well as a panel of senior or retired judges.

Would Too Many Judges and Justices Have to Recuse Themselves?

Given the proposed standards, it's possible that the enforcement of them would make it very hard for the judicial branch to function because so many judges would have an obligation to recuse themselves.

Take the Wisconsin Supreme Court. Many cases before it are brought by, or joined by, Wisconsin Manufacturers & Commerce. Now WMC has been one of the biggest outside groups to spend money on supreme court candidates, so all the justices who benefited from large expenditures by WMC would have to recuse themselves every time.

The proposal by the retired judges dealt with this problem by proposing an amendment to the Wisconsin Constitution to allow the state high court to appoint members of the appellate court to fill any vacancies caused by recusals in order to make a quorum.

That's an answer, but it's a long one. It would, like all amendments to our state constitution, require the passage of this proposal in two successive legislative sessions and then approval in a binding statewide referendum for it to take effect.

Here are a couple of other possible answers. First, we could go back to having public financing of Wisconsin Supreme Court elections, which would limit the problem on the high court. (Walker and the Republican-dominated legislature tossed that out soon after taking office.) We could also have full public financing for all our judicial contests. This would eliminate the possibility for, and the appearance of, corruption in every judicial branch.

Finally, even without public financing, it's possible that the new recusal rules would have the happy effect of deterring large donations and expenditures in judicial races. Wealthy and powerful special interests would know that if they threw their money around in judicial elections, the judges they "bought" would have to recuse themselves in any cases involving those interests.

That's a consummation devoutly to be wished.

chapter 7

Give Us Direct Democracy

It's early February 2011. Governor Scott Walker has just "dropped a bomb," to use his inelegant phrase: he's announced his intention to gut public sector unionism in Wisconsin with Act 10. In response, huge numbers of protesters are amassing at the Capitol Square. On subsequent weekends, the numbers reach one hundred thousand or more. And thousands fill the capitol itself and engage in a sleep-in that lasts three weeks. Eventually, the Capitol Police clear the capitol, and the leaders of the Democratic Party of Wisconsin and the state's biggest labor unions channel the energy of the protests into a move to recall Republican state senators, along with Walker.

Walker won his war against organized labor in Wisconsin, and he set an example for other Republican governors. Ohio governor John Kasich copied Walker's effort on March 31, 2011. Again, there were massive protests in that state's capitol. But in Ohio, the outcome was different because the citizens of Ohio had a swifter remedy than the recall: the Ohio Constitution allows citizens, by referendum, to veto a bill that the legislature and the governor have passed. Organizers got more than triple the number of signatures needed to put it on the ballot in November, and the voters of Ohio rejected the law by a whopping 62–38 margin.

So why couldn't Wisconsinites have used the same remedy?

Because, oddly, Wisconsin's constitution does not allow for binding referendums initiated by the citizenry. I say "oddly" because Wisconsin, under Fighting Bob La Follette, led the way in one progressive reform after another to empower voters, including having the voters—and not the party bosses—vote on who the candidates should be.

Progressives actually did champion the idea of the citizen initiative and referendum. Here is governor Francis McGovern in his 1911 message to the legislature: "The great task of the time is how to make and keep the government really representative of the people. The initiative [and] the referendum ... have been proposed as effective means for accomplishing this result," he said, adding that they "embody but one idea: that of placing the people in actual control of public affairs."

The voters of Wisconsin had an opportunity to amend the Wisconsin Constitution and grant themselves the powers of initiative and referendum. "In November 1914, the legislature placed on the ballot a constitutional amendment which would have given Wisconsin electors the initiative for constitutional amendments and state laws and would also have enabled voters to petition that a law already passed be submitted to a referendum vote before taking effect," a report by the Legislative Reference Bureau notes. But the citizens turned it down "by a vote of 148,536 to 84,934."

So why did the voters turn it down?

I found an answer at the website of the Initiative and Referendum Institute at the University of Southern California. "After 13 years in power, the Progressives had become overconfident. In the 1913 legislature, they passed a series of big tax increases to finance an ambitious public works program, as well as giving final approval to a constitutional amendment raising their salaries. This amendment went on the November 1914 ballot along with the I&R amendment and eight others," the Institute's profile on Wisconsin explains. "After paying the higher taxes in 1914, the voters had had their fill of the liberal reformers and all their works. The amendments on the 1914 ballot offered an easy target for the voters' wrath."

Over the years, according to the Legislative Reference Bureau, there have been "approximately 50 proposals" to grant to the voters the powers of the initiative and the referendum, but none have succeeded, even though twenty-six states have such powers.

Wisconsin is a laggard here.

SOLUTIONS

Several Democratic legislators have been trying to rectify this. In 2019, then representative David Crowley introduced a joint resolution to amend the constitution to state: "The people reserve to themselves the power of initiative to propose laws and to approve or reject those laws at an election independently of the legislature." Under his proposal, citizens would need to get petitions signed by "at least 5 percent of the vote cast for the office of secretary of state" in the preceding election.

"Too often," Crowley told me, "the politics of the capitol building get in the way of passing legislation that the majority of the people that we represent want. An initiative path to lawmaking allows the people to bypass the politics of the building and enact laws that are especially important to them. It doesn't undermine the legislative process—it enhances it."

In the same session of the legislature, representative Gary Hebl introduced a separate joint resolution that would grant initiative and referendum powers to the people of Wisconsin. Hebl's proposed referendum states: "The people reserve to themselves the power to approve or reject at a referendum any act of the Legislature or part of an act." It also states that no act may take effect for 120 days so that the citizens would have time to gather signatures for a referendum. Under Hebl's proposal, citizens would need to get petitions signed by "at least 4 percent of the vote cast for the office of governor" in the preceding election.

Hebl's referendum would also grant the initiative power to the people. It states: "The people reserve to themselves the power of initiative to propose laws and amendments to this constitution and to approve or reject them at an election." The signature hurdle is higher here: 6 percent of the vote cast for governor in the preceding election. Heble told me: "Citizens feel like 'I can't trust my legislator to get stuff done.' The people should decide the issues of the day. That's the way it should be done."

Representative Katrina Shankland, one of the cosponsors of Hebl's bill, says that if we had citizen initiative and referendum power, we already would have passed Medicaid expansion, universal registration of firearms, and medical marijuana—all of which have 80 percent or more public support.

But there is opposition in Wisconsin to letting the people express themselves, much less granting them the power of direct democracy.

Wisconsin Manufacturers & Commerce, a huge business lobby, released a report in December 2019 titled "Local (Out of) Control," in which it assailed even nonbinding referendums. "This type of activity raises many questions about how taxpayer funds are used, the openness of local government, and if the local citizenry are actually being appropriately represented," the report said.

Isn't it up to the local citizenry to decide whether they are being appropriately represented? And isn't having referendums one way to find that out?

But WMC is not alone in its hostility to hearing from the citizenry.

In December 2019, the Ozaukee County Board's lawyer said it was somehow illegal for the county to have a nonbinding referendum on banning gerrymandering. And that same month, Manitowoc county executive Bob Ziegelbauer vetoed a board decision to hold a nonbinding referendum on the gerrymandering issue.

As Shankland says, "There is a pattern of behavior of disrespect for their own constituents."

We need to break that pattern. We need to establish mechanisms for direct democracy in Wisconsin.

COUNTERARGUMENTS AND COMPLEXITIES

Direct Democracy Invites Rash Decisions and Negative Outcomes

Opponents of binding referendums tend to prefer the deliberative process of representative government rather than rule by the will of the people, which is what the initiative and referendum process provides.

The basic argument is that the voters might make rash decisions on complex issues that they not fully informed about or that might have highly negative consequences they didn't anticipate when they cast their ballots.

Two examples come quickly to mind.

The first is California's Proposition 13, a 1978 ballot initiative that passed almost two to one. Prop 13, as it became known, put a tight lid on any increases in property taxes. As a result, local governments were starved for money, as their tax revenues plummeted by 60 percent the very next year.

The second is Brexit, the decision by the British public in June 2016 to leave the European Union. The vote was a close one, 52–48, and immediately afterward, a sizable group of people who voted for it got a bad case of buyer's remorse and wished they had voted the other way, as the British pound sank and economic worries skyrocketed.

As Harvard economist Ken Rogoff put it after the Brexit vote: "The idea that somehow any decision reached anytime by majority rule is necessarily 'democratic' is a perversion of the term. This isn't democracy; it is Russian roulette for republics," he wrote in an op-ed for the *Boston Globe* (June 26, 2016) titled "Britain's Democratic Failure."

Certainly, as these critics note, there are risks that a majority of voters will make a foolish or dangerous choice when they vote on binding referendums. But those risks are inherent to democracy. Look, in my view, the voters made a foolish and dangerous choice when they voted for Donald Trump in 2016. But that doesn't mean they should be deprived of such a choice.

Either you believe in democracy or you don't. And when elected officials are routinely flouting the will of the people, as has been happening in Wisconsin for many years on many issues, you have to weigh that cost to democracy against the risk that the people will do something foolish. I, for one, am willing to take that risk.

Big Money Can Easily Get Its Way!

Another potential problem with the binding referendums is that big money and dark money can swoop in and try to buy the outcome they want with tons of advertising.

That was the case with Marsy's Law, the victims' rights amendment to the Wisconsin Constitution, which the voters ratified in 2020. This amendment was the brainchild not of any Wisconsinite but of California billionaire Henry Nicholas, the founder of Broadcom, who has spent $100 million across the country to get a dozen other states to amend their constitutions.

Here, Marsy's Law for Wisconsin spent $1.5 million in lobbying the legislature to get it passed in two consecutive sessions, as required by law. Amazingly, Marsy's Law for Wisconsin became the third biggest lobbyist in the state during this period, ranking right up there near WMC, even though Marsy's Law was working on only this one narrow issue.

During the referendum campaign, Marsy's Law for Wisconsin spared no expense. Its ads were everywhere—all over TV and radio and on your computer screen. The group even hired Kelsey Grammer to plug their cause.

Fortunately, circuit court judge Frank Remington tossed out Marsy's Law on November 3, 2020, ruling that Wisconsin voters were not properly informed that Marsy's Law would take away some of the fundamental rights of the accused as guaranteed in the Wisconsin Constitution.

So, yes, this is a serious risk, but again it is the same risk we face in our regular elections, where big and dark money dominate. The answer isn't to deprive voters of their right to the initiative process. The answer is to limit big and dark money.

chapter 8

Provide Ranked-Choice Voting

"As Maine goes, so goes the nation."

This old saying may take on new meaning, as Maine is leading the nation in experimenting with a new way to vote: it's called ranked-choice voting.

Here's how it works. On your ballot, you get to pick your first choice, and then you get to identify your second choice and your third choice. If one candidate gets a majority of the votes, that candidate wins, just as in the current system. But if no candidate gets a majority, then the candidate with the fewest first-place votes is eliminated, and those who voted for that candidate then get to have their second-choice candidate counted as their first choice. This process continues until one candidate gets a majority of the votes.

In Maine, in 2018, this process actually elected a member of Congress. And the process resulted in a different person being elected than the one who would have been victorious under the traditional way of voting.

Republican incumbent Bruce Poliquin and Democrat Jared Golden ran neck and neck in Maine's Second Congressional District. On election night, Poliquin ended up being ahead by 2,107 votes out of a total of 266,015. But he didn't have a majority; he had 46.3 percent of the vote. Two independent candidates, Will Hoar and Tiffany Bond, combined for about 8 percent of the vote. The second-choice preferences of the Hoar and Bond voters were then counted, and Golden received a lot more of their second-choice votes than Poliquin. As a result, Golden won on the reallocation by 2,905 votes.

One benefit of ranked-choice voting (which used to be called instant-runoff voting) is that the person who wins more accurately reflects the sentiments of the voting public. More people in Maine, for instance, actually preferred Golden to Poliquin, as it turned out.

Another benefit of ranked-choice voting is that it eliminates the "spoiler effect." Under our traditional system, if you vote for a third-party or Independent candidate who is closest to your way of thinking, you run the risk of letting your least favorite candidate win a plurality of votes. You'll recall that Bush won Florida (with a big assist from the US Supreme Court) by a margin of 537 votes. You'll also recall that Ralph Nader won 97,421 votes in Florida as the Green Party candidate. If Florida had ranked-choice voting and if most of those Nader voters had chosen Gore as their second pick, Gore would have won.

Ranked-choice voting is especially useful in crowded primary fields. Just think of the Republican presidential primaries in 2016, or the Democrat presidential primaries in 2020, or the Democratic primary for governor in Wisconsin in 2018. If you had ranked-choice voting in those primaries, the candidates who had the most first-place and second-place votes combined might have emerged more quickly as the front-runner, or there may even have been a different winner altogether.

By the way, it's not just Maine that is using ranked-choice voting. Australia and New Zealand use it. So do Ireland and Malta. Democracies all.

In the United States, an increasing number of cities and towns are using it for municipal or school board elections, including Berkeley, Cambridge, Minneapolis, Oakland, Portland (Maine), San Francisco, Santa Fe, St. Paul, and Takoma Park, among others.

Unfortunately, in Wisconsin, cities and towns probably would be prohibited from using ranked-choice voting because the state's authority over elections would supersede any local effort. "Because state law provides a comprehensive scheme for the administration of all elections within this state (as well as a state agency that oversees these elections), it would seem likely that a court . . . would not allow cities or villages to use their home rule authority to enact by local ordinance an alternate method of counting votes and determining a winner," according to a January 25, 2019, memorandum from the Legislative Reference Bureau to senator Chris Larson.

SOLUTIONS

There's a movement afoot in Wisconsin to change this. It's being led by Milwaukee businesswoman Katherine Gehl and her organization, Democracy Found, as well as by local members of national groups like Fair Vote,

Represent Us, and Unite America. Gehl is the former president and CEO of Gehl Foods in Milwaukee.

In the legislature in 2019, representative Mark Spreitzer and then senator Mark Miller introduced bills to allow ranked-choice voting in all elections in Wisconsin except for recalls.

"Ranked-choice voting is an innovative and practical way to make sure people can vote for who they truly want, rather than vote strategically for who they think has the best chance of winning," Spreitzer said in a press release. "Ranked-choice voting also ensures that those who serve in elected office are there because they have the support of a clear majority of voters."

Miller added: "Ranked-choice voting gives voters the best opportunity to elect representation with the broadest public support."

"It's something I've been personally interested in for a long time," Spreitzer told me. "I studied comparative elective systems in college." He went to Beloit College and represents the Beloit area. "I've certainly had some constituents, including a former professor, support this idea," he says, "and as the State of Maine has moved to this, there's been a lot more public awareness of it."

Spreitzer says he feels for voters who tell him, "I'd like to vote Libertarian, Green, or Independent, but one of the two major candidates is going to win, and I don't want throw my vote away." Ranked-choice voting solves that dilemma, he says.

In the Republican presidential primaries back in 2016, where Donald Trump was pulling 40 percent of the vote but everyone else was divvying up the anti-Trump vote, ranked-choice voting might have led to a different outcome, Spreitzer says, sparing us a Trump presidency.

Spreitzer and Miller also noted that ranked-choice voting would save taxpayers some money. It "would eliminate the need for the nonpartisan February primary," the press release noted. In February 2020, for instance, three candidates were running in the nonpartisan-in-name-only primary for Wisconsin Supreme Court, and the top two candidates went on to the general election. But since ranked-choice voting automatically reallocates votes until one person has a majority anyway, we could have skipped that primary entirely and elected a justice in the general election, even with three candidates.

Spreitzer recognizes that the prospects for the bill may not be great at the moment. Still, he's upbeat about the long term and about getting support from across the aisle. "It's a conversation starter," he says, adding, "I'm hopeful."

COUNTERARGUMENTS AND COMPLEXITIES
Some Voters Would Be Left Out

The Heritage Foundation, one of the leading right-wing think tanks in the country, published a critique on April 23, 2019, titled "Ranked-Choice Voting Is a Bad Choice," by Hans von Spakovsky and J. Adams. "Second- or third-choice votes should not matter in America," the authors wrote. "They do not provide the mandate that ensures that the representatives in a republic have the confidence and support of a majority of the public in the legitimacy of their decisions."

But the whole point of ranked-choice voting is to not get stuck with someone who won without the "support of a majority of the public."

Spakovsky and Adams did make a more interesting argument, though. They claimed that ranked-choice voting can end up disenfranchising those voters who don't rank all the candidates on their ballot.

"If a voter only ranks two of the five candidates and those two are eliminated in the first and second rounds of tabulation, their choices will not be considered in the remaining rounds of tabulation," they wrote. This "disenfranchises voters, because ballots that do not include the two ultimate finalists are cast aside to manufacture a faux majority for the winner. . . . You, as a voter, are not given the opportunity to make the final decision between competing substitutes."

Simon Waxman in the progressive journal *Democracy* (November 3, 2016) made the same argument. "Say there are five candidates running," he wrote, "but the voter ranks only three, and all three are eliminated prior to the last round. As a result, none of their votes will have gone to the winning candidate or the runner-up. In effect, their ballot doesn't figure in the outcome."

But if you're voting for a third-party candidate or an Independent with little chance of winning and you don't have ranked-choice voting, you're also giving up any opportunity to weigh in on the two likeliest winners. That seems worse than the disenfranchisement that Spakovsky and Adams posit, which isn't disenfranchisement at all, since everyone had the chance to vote and to list their favorites, in order.

Katherine Gehl's Top-Five Idea

Democracy Found is dedicated to "revitalizing America's voting process" and thereby "revitalizing our democracy." Gehl's vision of ranked-choice voting comes with a couple of twists: she seeks to use it in combination with the nonpartisan elimination primaries, and then she wants ranked-choice voting among the top five candidates in the nonpartisan primary. Instead of voting on the Democratic side or the Republican side during primaries, voters would vote for only one candidate from all the candidates running. In Gehl's proposal, the candidates who were in the top five would then run in the general election, which would be decided by ranked-choice voting.

"The combination of top-five primaries and ranked-choice voting in general elections will help restore healthy political competition in the public interest," she says. "With healthy competition, Washington will be incented to address our greatest challenges."

Her group also argues that this innovative process would "reduce partisanship because candidates must appeal to a majority of voters." It also, the group says, would lead to "more positive campaigns" because candidates would need to appeal to people's second or third choices, and if you're running a negative campaign, you're going to turn people off.

The result, the group says on its website, is that "the candidate with the broadest appeal wins."

One practical problem with this combo proposal is that it multiplies the hurdles. It may be hard enough to get ranked-choice voting by itself, but it's going to be doubly hard to do away with partisan primaries when so many people identify with one party or another, and when the officials of each party—and their power brokers—wield so much influence. And then it could be triply hard to bring people around to her top-five concept.

On the merits, there are these questions: Do you always want "the candidate with the broadest appeal" to win? Might it be better to have a principled candidate with a narrower base but a larger vision win?

Actually, Spakovsky and Adams waved at this problem in their Heritage Foundation report when they said that ranked-choice voting "obscures true debates and issue-driven dialogues" and tilts the field toward the more "generic" candidate.

Take the Bernie Sanders campaign in 2020. For a while there, it looked like he was going to get the nomination in a crowded field by winning a sizable plurality of the votes going into the Democratic convention. He certainly wasn't the most generic candidate, and he didn't go out of his way to broaden his appeal, so he might not have won if there were ranked-choice voting. But he was the visionary candidate, and he almost pulled it off.

With ranked-choice voting, especially coupled with nonpartisan primaries, a visionary candidate may be at a disadvantage, and the country would suffer by not getting the ideas or leadership of that candidate.

The Benefits Are Overblown

In his *Democracy* article, Waxman minimized the value of the ranked-choice voting reform. "It is not a bad thing if RCV enables no-guilt third-party voting," he wrote, "but doing so won't wrest power from Democrats and Republicans and turn it over to independents."

To substantiate his point, Waxman turned to Australia, which has used ranked-choice voting for many years. "In the 2013 Australian federal election, 90 percent of constituencies elected the candidate with the most first-preference votes, which suggests that choice ranking had little effect on the outcome," he writes. "And it is hard to ignore the resemblance between the Australian and U.S. governments, as far as partisan divisions go. Despite RCV, just two governments have led in Australia for almost the entire history of the current Federal Parliament: Labor and Liberal-National . . . federal election in Australia, one of the two major parties wins, RCV be damned."

To the extent that advocates of ranked-choice voting make the claim that more independents will get elected this way, Waxman has a point. But that's not the main argument on the ranked-choice voting side. Rather, it's to arrive at a choice that a majority supports.

Waxman makes a further, more sweeping point: ranked-choice voting is a technical reform that doesn't get at the heart of the democracy problem in the United States: legislators are "doing the bidding of donors" and not serving their constituents. Waxman derides ranked-choice voting as "technical meddling."

He concludes: "None of this is to say that RCV is sure to be hazardous. Maybe it is even an experiment worth trying. But it is notable that . . . concerned citizens are looking to procedural minutiae as their savior."

I'd say it's worth trying. But if you put a gun to my head, I would say, Let's solve the money in politics problem first, along with some other biggies, like uprooting racism and moving toward economic democracy.

chapter 9

Restore Local Control

In the summer of 2018, I was on a couple of panels in western Wisconsin about the assault on home rule and local control in Wisconsin. With me on the panels, which drew several dozen citizens, was Dennis Brault, chair of the Vernon County Board, and Tara Johnson, chair of the La Crosse County Board.

Johnson pointed out how outrageous it was that the La Crosse County Board no longer had the authority to limit the location of cell towers, even if they were in scenic spots on the bluffs above the Mississippi River.

Brault spoke broadly, saying that the Republican leadership in the legislature has been "taking away the right of our cities, villages, and towns to enact ordinances that protect the health, safety, appearance, and lifestyles of their communities."

It used to be that the cry for "local control" came from Republicans or Dixiecrat Democrats who didn't want to enforce civil rights legislation. But over the past decade, as corporate special interests have interfered with local self-governments, many county board leaders and some Democratic legislators have bemoaned the loss of local control.

Philosophically, the reason for local control in a democracy is simple: we, in our local communities, know what's best for us, and the local officials we elect are so close to us, the citizens, that we can't be ignored. They see us when they shop for groceries, when they go to the hardware store, and when they worship or exercise. And when we run into them, we can give them an earful if we don't like what they're doing.

In Wisconsin, the fight for local democracy was part of the Progressive movement's agenda. The legislature passed a home rule bill in 1911, and it was signed into law by governor Francis McGovern, who was a La Follette Republican. A year later, however, the Wisconsin Supreme Court threw the law out, so advocates of home rule set about amending the Wisconsin Constitution, which they achieved in 1924. That amendment reads: "Cities and villages organized pursuant to state law are hereby empowered to determine their local affairs and government, subject only to this constitution and to such enactments of the legislature of state-wide concern as shall with uniformity affect every city or every village. The method of such determination shall be prescribed by the legislature."

Courts have limited this power over the past ninety-seven years, as have governors and legislatures. Republican Tommy Thompson imposed limits on the levying authority of local governments. And Democrat Jim Doyle signed two disastrous bills that encroached on local control. The first, in 2003, limited the ability of local governments to ban factory farms. And the second, just a year later, prohibited local governments from raising the minimum wage above the level set by the state. That's why we still have a paltry $7.25 minimum wage all across Wisconsin. Madison and Milwaukee would long ago have raised the minimum wage in their cities if Doyle had not signed that bill into law.

But governor Scott Walker and senate majority leader Scott Fitzgerald and assembly speaker Robin Vos took the assault on local democracy to new and dangerous heights. They passed more than 180 bills that interfere with local self-government.

Here are some of the ways they curtailed local democracy:

- They prohibited local governments from requiring employers to offer paid sick leave, overturning a pathbreaking Milwaukee ordinance.
- They passed numerous antilabor laws that prohibit local governments from negotiating benefits (Act 10) with unions, or from requiring prevailing wages on contracts or from establishing higher employment benefits or living wages on local government contracts.
- They passed a slew of pro-landlord bills, including one that prohibits local governments from inspecting properties for a landlord's first eight years of ownership and from reinspecting properties for another five years if the landlord fixed any problems that were identified.
- They passed a law prohibiting local governments from imposing their own insurance requirements on pipeline companies.

- They passed a law curbing local control over the siting of cell phone towers.
- They passed a law prohibiting local governments from forcing banks to sell "zombie" properties in a timely fashion.
- They passed a law prohibiting local governments from enacting tougher shoreland zoning laws than the state.
- They passed a law prohibiting counties from enacting a development moratorium.
- They passed a law prohibiting communities from banning or restricting bow-and-arrow and crossbow hunting.
- They even passed a law prohibiting counties from helping out cities on building projects.

So why has there been this soup-to-nuts assault on local control from the leaders of the Republican Party, which used to be the party of local control but is now, as my predecessor Mike McCabe says, "the party that controls the locals"?

Because, in a fundamental way, the leaders of the Republican Party are in hock to their donors. From 2011 to 2018, Walker and Fitzgerald and Vos weren't really running Wisconsin. They were the water boys for the people and groups that were actually running Wisconsin.

Chief among them were:

- Wisconsin Manufacturers & Commerce (WMC), which spent more than $20 million to keep them in power.
- the Koch brothers and their group Americans for Prosperity, which spent almost $8 million to keep them in power.
- Betsy Devos's school privatization group, American Federation for Children, which spent $6.5 million to keep them in power.

These are the folks who were running Wisconsin. And they don't like democracy because it interferes with their ability to maximize profits. So they do what they can to limit democracy. And it's easier—it's more efficient—for them to buy up the governor and the legislature than it is to buy up every single local governmental body.

We are seeing in Wisconsin, and we are seeing nationally, this battle between self-government and corporate government, this battle between democracy and oligarchy.

This is an old struggle. As Thomas Jefferson warned us, two hundred years ago: "We must crush in its birth the aristocracy of our monied corporations."

But they're not in their cribs any longer. They're fully grown now; in fact, they're giant monsters trampling all over our democracy.

Fighting Bob La Follette tangled with these monsters a hundred years ago. Corporate dominance over our democracy was his overriding concern. And he would be appalled today, but maybe not surprised, to see corporations with the upper hand.

Shortly before he died, La Follette wrote: "Reaction is in the saddle, and it will ride with whip and spur."

Well, reaction is now flogging our democracy.

Here's an example: WMC came out with a report on December 10, 2019, to pressure the legislature to limit the ability of local governments to do lobbying. The report, titled "Local (Out of) Control," wants the legislature to pass a law that "prohibits local governments from using taxpayer funds to hire private entities that lobby state government."

WMC wants to tie the hands of local governments from hiring lobbyists to advocate for their interests and at least try to combat the outsized influence of WMC. Essentially, in a duel with local governments, WMC wants to disarm its opponents.

Not that it's being outgunned.

In the 2017–18 legislative session, WMC was the biggest lobbyist in the state, spending $1.4 million. The Wisconsin Counties Association (WCA), which it singles out for criticism, spent $800,000. In the first six months of 2019, WMC spent $414,000 on lobbying, and WCA spent $249,000.

Nevertheless, WMC alleges that associations and private lobbyists hired by local governments often "advocate against the best interest of taxpayers." It doesn't say that they also advocate against the special interests of big corporations, but WMC does note that "Wisconsin CEOs ranked this as the top issue to pursue in a recent WMC survey."

A glance at the WCA's 2019–20 legislative agenda offers clues about the animosity of WMC. Items on that agenda include "protect groundwater from contamination and overuse," "close the dark store property assessment loophole," and "increase funding for mass transit"—all of which WMC opposes.

Fortunately, representative Katrina Shankland of Stevens Point is leading the effort in the legislature to shore up local control. She's the one who asked the Legislative Reference Bureau to come up with a study on the number of bills that have been passed that curbed local control.

"For the state legislature to neuter the ability of local elected officials to govern their communities isn't just frustrating," she told me. "It's disenfranchising."

Shankland links the attack on local control with partisan gerrymandering. "When you combine gerrymandering with the erosion of local control, people feel like their voice is not heard at all," she says. "The intent, and the effect, is to discourage and completely demotivate voters, so they say, 'My voice doesn't matter. And if my voice doesn't matter, why should I call my legislator? Why should I even vote?' The ultimate goal is to make people feel like it's futile to fight back."

Shankland was encouraged when she heard about the turnout at the panels I was on, and she also noticed that the issue is gaining momentum at the grassroots level.

"More and more people are looking at this issue of local control," she says. "Once people see the number of bills—more than 180!—that were passed limiting local control, that's powerful."

SOLUTIONS

Shankland is trying to roll back, bit by bit, the limits that the legislature has imposed. She cites the bill that the legislature passed to prohibit municipalities from restricting, regulating, or taxing the use of plastic bags. "The City of Stevens Point had drafted an ordinance to ban plastic bags after a lot of activists had urged their alders to back it," she explains. "It was citizen democracy in action. But that same week, I had to tell the alders that the state legislature was taking their ability to regulate plastic bags away, and they couldn't do anything about it."

Shankland introduced a bill in 2019 to repeal this prohibition on municipalities that want to ban or impose regulations on bags and containers that are "designed for transporting or protecting merchandise, food or beverages from a food service or retail facility."

It's a small case, which she hasn't won yet. But it shows how deeply the legislature has dug its claws into local community affairs.

The larger issue of local control needs to gain even more popular support, across party lines, for it to succeed, Shankland says.

"We need to continue to push on this issue," Shankland says. "The state needs to stop tying the hands of local government."

COUNTERARGUMENTS AND COMPLEXITIES
Local Control Is Bad for Business

Businesses that operate statewide find it costly and burdensome to comply with a variety of different regulations that counties or local municipalities enact. It's much simpler for them if there's just one set of regulations for the whole state.

For instance, in 2018, the Republican-dominated legislature rejected the ability of local governments to engage in "labor peace agreements," or to have requirements on overtime hours that are stricter than state law, or even to prohibit employers from asking prospective employees about their previous salaries.

"Supporters of the bill contended it will help remove burdensome regulation," Laurel White and Shawn Johnson reported for Wisconsin Public Radio on February 22, 2018. They quoted Republican representative John Nygren as saying: "If you want to continue to over-regulate an industry that's about opportunity, have at it. But don't count me in."

Nationwide, the push to preempt or usurp local control has been led by the American Legislative Exchange Council (ALEC), a powerful group of big business interests and conservative state legislators that come up with "model" legislation. "ALEC's guiding principle—supporting big business— turns the small-c conservative ideal of individual liberty and local control on its head," wrote Democratic state representative Chris Taylor for *The Progressive*'s website on May 13, 2014. Taylor attended several ALEC meetings. At one, Utah state senator Howard Stephenson was quite blunt: "We need to stomp out local control," he said, according to Taylor. He added that school boards and city councils take away liberties quicker than the federal government. As Taylor concluded: "Local governing entities can be a roadblock to the ALEC agenda, so their power needs to be preempted and removed."

Republican leaders in Wisconsin aren't as blunt as Stephenson. *Journal Sentinel* reporter Molly Beck in 2016 asked Speaker Vos about this, and he answered: Republicans—typically champions of less government and autonomy of local governments—still hold those values as priorities but "once in a while a statewide standard makes more sense."

Of course, 180 times is more than once in a while, and dozens of those bills closely resembled ALEC bills.

But what about the merits of the argument? While you can understand the perspective of the business person, basically, the issue boils down to this: do we have local self-government, or not? If a local community can't block a cell tower from being built on a scenic bluff, or can't say how often a landlord can be inspected, or what the overtime rules are for local public employees, why even bother with the fiction of local self-rule?

And if the regulations imposed by local governments are so antibusiness that they're going to send companies elsewhere and lead to higher local unemployment, that's a consequence that citizens can rectify, if they want to, at the voting booth.

Local Control Opens the Door to Jim Crow

Certainly, sixty years ago, the phrase "local control" was a rallying cry of segregationists in the South, like Lester Maddox, Strom Thurmond, and George Wallace, just as it was in the post-Reconstruction period. And we saw what happened after the *Shelby County* decision of 2013 by the US Supreme Court, which gutted the Voting Rights Act by relieving southern states of the need for "preclearance" before they could change their voting procedures. Almost before the ink was dry on this decision, one state after another started to erect obstacles on the way to the voting booth.

They were acting, you could say, under the rubric of local control. But by "local control," I don't mean that local communities have the right to take away anybody's fundamental rights, which is what these states have been doing. Local control is about a community governing its own affairs so long as its rules don't infringe on people's fundamental rights. Regulating the placement of cell towers, for instance, is no such infringement.

What about Local Control of Public Education?

Another tricky example is public education. Many states have equalized their funding across school districts so that kids in poor districts don't get less funding than kids in rich districts. Is this an assault on local control, and if so, how is it justified, in contrast with others?

Again, the answer comes down to fundamental rights. Equity in public education is a fundamental right, and equality of opportunity is a fundamental precept of our society. There is no equity, and there is no equality of opportunity, if a student in a rich district is getting many more resources than a student in a poor district.

But the issue of local control and public education gets even more entangled when you go into the curriculum thicket. In Texas in 2009, the state board of education required schools to teach "all sides" of theories explaining the origins of life on Earth—a way to bring creationism back in the classroom.

A few years later, in 2015, it approved a geography textbook that whitewashed the slave trade, saying that it brought "millions of workers from Africa to the southern United States to work on agricultural plantations."

Should state boards of education, should local school boards, have the right to instruct their students in creationism or to offer racist characterizations of slavery?

"There should be a warning label with radical local control," Tim Slekar, dean of the School of Education at Edgewood College, told me. "Public education is not just for those living within local boundaries. It's universal. It's for cultivating democratic citizenship."

The principle is that local control can be preempted only when it is denying people's fundamental rights, and equity in education is one of those.

And if you want to argue about what's fundamental, let's have at it. That's what our democracy is for.

chapter 10

Save Local Media

It's October 7, 2019, three days before a big press conference on banning gerrymandering that our Fair Maps Coalition is hosting in Marshfield. I'm on the web looking for emails and phone numbers of reporters in Marshfield. I find the *Marshfield News-Herald* website. It lists only four reporters, and only one who covers public issues. I email her and get this: "I will be on vacation until Monday, October 14. If you need immediate assistance, you can email news@wisconsinrapidstribunecom or news@marshfieldnews herald.com."

I try news@marshfieldnewsherald.com, and the email doesn't go through.

I go back to the website of the *Marshfield News-Herald* to contact the editor. I discover that the title of the editor is not "editor" or "editor in chief" but "content coach." The name under that title is Jamie Rokus, who is also the "content coach" at the *Wausau Daily Herald*.

I shoot Rokus an email. No response.

Not to be deterred, I contact reporters directly at the Wausau paper and at a couple of the Wausau TV stations, a little more than an hour away.

Fortunately, two of them show up for our press conference at 10 a.m. on October 10: Laura Schulte from the *Wausau Daily Herald* and Naomi Kowles from WSAW-TV. I'm grateful they made the drive.

But I'm left wondering about the *Marshfield News-Herald*, so I ask one of the local speakers at the press conference, Chris Jockheck. He's a former mayor of Marshfield and is back on the city council, by night—by day, he's a carpenter.

"Chris, what's up with the *Marshfield News-Herald*? I couldn't get anyone from the paper to come today," I say.

"It's a ghost paper," Jockheck told me. "It's just a logo on a paper that's produced out of Wausau. They don't have a staff to speak of here. No one comes to our city council meetings anymore. It's a disaster! The public has no way of getting the information they need about what's going on here."

Two months later, I called Jockheck back, and he told me he picked up the *Marshfield News-Herald* and the *Wausau Daily Herald* that morning. "The Marshfield paper is the same as the Wausau paper. There are different obituaries, but every single story that appears in the Marshfield paper is in the Wausau paper. None of them are about Marshfield. But things do happen here. We have 15,000 to 20,000 people here and a large medical complex, the Marshfield Clinic. We have a 400-bed hospital with 400 docs."

But no daily paper, in reality. "Twenty years ago, this was a locally produced paper," Jockheck says. "I knew the publisher, who lived down the street. I knew the editor. I knew the reporters. Now I'm not even sure there's an office here except for advertising."

The *Marshfield News-Herald* is part of Gannett's *USA Today* network of eleven Wisconsin papers, including the flagship *Milwaukee Journal Sentinel*. (The other papers are the *Appleton Post-Crescent*, *Green Bay Press-Gazette*, *Fond du Lac Reporter*, *Wausau Daily Herald*, *Stevens Point Journal*, *Sheboygan Press*, *Oshkosh Northwestern*, *Manitowoc Herald Times Reporter*, and *Wisconsin Rapids Daily Tribune*.) That network had already done away with a lot of local reporters when it was bought up by GateHouse Media and its owner, New Media Investment Group, in August 2019.

Bruce Murphy, the editor of *Urban Milwaukee*, predicts that this will lead to the mergers of some of the papers and an "even greater de-emphasis on local journalism because it doesn't drive big traffic numbers, which the company will desperately need to drive revenue."

"GateHouse isn't a newspaper company. It's a hedge fund," agrees Lew Friedland, UW–Madison professor in the School of Journalism and Mass Communication, who founded and directs the Center for Communication and Democracy. "It makes money by cutting reporters and by cutting the newshole. As GateHouse takes over, these ghost newspapers will absolutely grow. There will be more news deserts, less local news coverage, and less coverage of the statehouse."

Already, at least nine counties in Wisconsin have no daily newspaper, according to the *Columbia Journalism Review*. Those counties are Adams, Ashland, Bayfield, Douglas, Iron, Langlade, Oneida, Rusk, and Taylor. Their combined population comes to 191,651 people without a daily newspaper in their counties.

Friedland believes there may be several more counties that don't have a daily newspaper, and that the number will continue to grow. "As bad as that is, equally bad is the existence of the ghost papers with a company that pretends to be covering local news but is just sucking money out of the local economy," he told me.

This is not healthy for democracy.

"The stakes are high," says a 2018 study by the University of North Carolina's School of Media and Journalism titled "The Expanding News Desert." "Our sense of community and our trust in democracy at all levels suffer when journalism is lost or diminished. . . . The fate of communities across the country—and of grassroots democracy itself—is linked to the vitality of local journalism."

When citizens don't have reliable information about what their locally elected officials are actually doing, they're unable to hold them to account. And when citizens have no reliable way of finding out about how special interests are throwing their weight around to get favors, the potential for corruption rises toxically.

These trends are especially disempowering for those who have traditionally been left out. "The people with the least access to local news," the report notes, "are often the most vulnerable—the poorest, least educated and most isolated." It adds: "Metro, regional and state papers have dramatically scaled back their coverage of city neighborhoods, the suburbs and rural areas."

As John Nichols and Robert McChesney, authors of *The Death and Life of American Journalism*, noted in *The Nation* magazine way back in 2009, "Politicians and administrators will work increasingly without independent scrutiny and without public accountability. We are entering historically uncharted territory in America, a country that from its founding has valued the press not merely as a watchdog but as the essential nurturer of an informed citizenry. The collapse of journalism and the democratic infrastructure it sustains is not a development that anyone, except perhaps corrupt politicians and the interests they serve, looks forward to."

Ten years later, Nichols, who's the associate editor of the *Capital Times* in Madison, gave a dreary assessment of journalism in Wisconsin. In an interview in the summer of 2019 with Ruth Conniff, executive editor of the Wisconsin Examiner, Nichols said:

I would submit that Wisconsin, a state that historically benefitted from a great deal of diverse and contentious journalism, has seen the worst of it. These losses are across the board: in print, broadcast and online. . . . By some estimates, as many as 1 in 5 Americans now live in news deserts, and the problem is rapidly growing worse.

Cuts in the coverage of low-income and working-class communities are a huge issue. They make it harder to tackle inequality, to identify environmental racism, to preserve services, and to maintain robust democracy. And the damage is compounded by cuts in statehouse coverage.

The Wisconsin Center for Investigative Journalism, run by Andy and Dee Hall, fills some of this void, though its staff is small. "Thank God for the Wisconsin Center for Investigative Journalism," says Friedland. "Without it, the level of watchdog coverage would be hanging by a thread and subject to the whims of GateHouse and a few others."

Independent online publications like *Urban Milwaukee* are filling some of the void, though on a shoestring.

Wisconsin Public Radio and TV also play a positive role, says Friedland: "They've always fought way above their weight. WPR does a great job, and WPT's weekly statewide show is really good." But they could do more. "In the best of all possible worlds, you'd have WPT doing modest nightly newscasts," Friedland says.

"We think we're a part of the solution," says Mike Crane, director of Wisconsin Public Radio. "One of the things we're all worried about is the development of news deserts. The only daily news that's coming out of Superior is whatever we're doing. There isn't a daily newspaper that's based in Superior anymore."

A side note on WPR: When I travel around Wisconsin, I get a lot of feedback from listeners who wish that the Ideas Network would reinstitute its Friday week-in-review program. Running from 8 a.m. to 9 a.m., it used to feature a commentator from the right and a commentator from the left (I was on occasionally, representing the left). There are just too few places in Wisconsin these days where we can have civil dialogue across the ideological divide, and this was one of them. Compounding the problem, the biggest newspaper in the state, the *Journal Sentinel*, doesn't even have an op-ed or commentary page anymore.

"Public media is the space for that kind of thing," says Friedland. "In this day and age, it's a critical function."

Without this shared public space, ideological competitors are getting into the act. RightWisconsin's website furnishes conservative commentary and coverage on almost a daily basis. From the other side is the Wisconsin Examiner, which launched in the summer of 2019. Run by Conniff, a former editor of *The Progressive* magazine, and Melanie Conklin, a veteran of *Isthmus* and of US representative Mark Pocan's staff, Wisconsin Examiner is a news website with fresh daily content. There is also UpNorthNews, which bills itself as a "progressive news site" that is trying to make up for "the decline of local and state news coverage from traditional media outlets."

On talk radio, which is overwhelmingly right-wing in Wisconsin, as elsewhere, Michael Crute has pioneered progressive talk radio in Madison and, for a while, in Milwaukee, and is eager to expand statewide.

These competitors, however, may reinforce the increasing sense that people are living in two parallel media universes. Righties can listen to Sean Hannity and his ilk on the radio, and can be connected like an IV drip to Fox News all day and all night. And lefties can tune in to *Democracy Now!*, listen to Progressive talk radio, and watch MSNBC 24/7. Meanwhile, Facebook's algorithms constantly feed you the perspective you already like.

Living in an echo chamber doesn't build understanding, much less empathy, for those who don't see the world the way you do. It also can make you intellectually flabby because you never have to wrestle with an opinion that conflicts with your own.

SOLUTIONS

"We need a Marshall Plan for local media," says Craig Aaron, executive director of the national nonprofit group Free Press. "Journalism is in crisis, and what we need is largely incompatible with the commercial model."

Aaron says New Jersey, of all places, is leading the way. In 2018, it passed a law creating the New Jersey Civic Information Consortium. (The New Jersey senate passed it by a whopping 35–1.) "The people of New Jersey need accurate, relevant, timely, and trustworthy news and information to be civically engaged, make informed voting decisions, and work toward common solutions in their communities," the law states. The consortium, which consists of five public universities in the state, is designed "to advance research and innovation in the field of media and technology to better inform the State's communities to benefit the State's civic life and evolving information needs." The state has allocated up to $2 million to the consortium already.

Wisconsin should create a similar consortium right here. But reviving journalism, in Wisconsin and across the country, will require more fundamental changes.

"You have to build an entire new infrastructure of nonprofit news," says Friedland. "Publicly supported nonprofit news is going to have to replace commercial news if we're going to have a safe and secure flow of local news."

Aaron puts it this way: "It boils down to public investments."

Victor Pickard, an associate professor at the Annenberg School for Communication at the University of Pennsylvania, agrees with Aaron. Pickard codirects the Media, Inequality, and Change Center there and in 2019 published an important book, *Democracy without Journalism?*

The United States lags behind a lot of industrialized countries in its public funding of media, Pickard notes. "Whereas Japan, Britain, and Northern European countries spend anywhere from $50 to well over $100 per capita on public media, the United States government allocates about $1.40 per person per year," he writes.

Pickard advocates for increased public funding not just for PBS and NPR but also for "low-power FM stations and other community stations, public-access cable television, independent community news sites, and other local outlets." He envisions "transitioning them into multimedia centers," which "could combine their collective resources . . . to collaborate on the local and investigative reporting that is no longer covered by collapsing commercial newspapers." He adds: "An even more ambitious plan would transform existing infrastructure, such as post offices and public libraries, into local community centers."

If we had even a fraction of those reforms in place, we might finally be able to find out what's actually happening at the Marshfield city council meetings—and a whole lot more.

COUNTERARGUMENTS AND COMPLEXITIES

Public Subsidies Would Violate the First Amendment

This is a common argument against government support for independent media. It was made again by Nick Gillespie, who was editor in chief of the libertarian magazine *Reason* from 2000 to 2008 and Reason.com for another ten years. In an article for Reason.com on August 27, 2019, he took aim at senator Bernie Sanders for proposing government subsidies for independent journalism.

The day before, an op-ed by Sanders appeared on *Columbia Journalism Review*'s website about the desperate need to support independent newspapers and to "fund nonprofit civic-minded media. That will be part of an overall effort to substantially increase funding for programs that support public media's news-gathering operations at the local level—in much the same way many other countries already fund independent public media."

In Gillespie's retort, titled "Bernie Sanders' Plan to Save Newspapers Is Wrong on Every Level," he said it would be "an unprecedented power grab over freedom of speech and the press."

Just about every time the subject of public support for the media comes up, this counterargument is thrown in our face.

But media scholar Robert McChesney has spent a large part of his career debunking this argument. "The Founders provided massive printing and postal subsidies to spawn newspapers the market would have never countenanced," he wrote in "Freedom of the Press for Whom?" for the *Hofstra Law Review* in 2007. He added: "The press was seen not as a business enterprise but as a quasi-formal and indispensable branch of government, the Fourth Estate."

What's more, throughout its development, the media has developed along the lines that it did because of the "centrality of government policies" that supported it, McChesney wrote. "The media and communication systems in the United States have been the recipients of enormous direct and indirect subsidies, arguably as great as or greater than any other industry in our economy," he continued. "So the question is not whether we will have subsidies and policies, but, rather, what will be the subsidies and policies and what institutions will they support and what values will they encourage and promote?"

McChesney acknowledged that this is a complicated area. "This is nothing if not a complex matter," he wrote. "The problem of establishing a press system, providing direct and indirect subsidies, yet preventing censorship and state domination defies simple solution. And there may be no ideal solution, only a range of solutions where some are better than others."

He has noted, in subsequent books and articles, that many advanced industrial democracies have managed to implement some of these solutions without infringing on freedom of the press.

It's Not Necessary because of the Internet

Another common argument, which Gillespie also touched on, claims that because of the internet, "nobody is suffering from a lack of ideologically diverse and in-depth information about every possible topic under the sun. There may well be more chaff mixed in with the wheat, but that's because we now have far more choice of what to read."

While there certainly is a lot more out there, and while it's true that the barriers to entry are low now for anybody who owns a computer or a cell phone, that doesn't mean, by any stretch, that we've got plenty of "in-depth information" on everything under the sun. Sure, there are plenty of opinions out there. But there's not nearly enough reporting—actual reporting!—at the village, town, city, county, and state levels. Nor do many people on their phones and computers have the resources to spend on painstaking investigative reporting.

To deny that there's a news desert is to bury one's head in the internet.

The Government Shouldn't Fund Any Media

This argument, led by libertarians and right-wing Republicans such as Rand Paul, comes up perennially around budget time. For instance, in "Why It's Time to End Government-Funded Media," Bill Wirtz, a fellow at the free-enterprise think tank the Foundation for Economic Education, wrote on its website (October 2, 2018), "When we deprive citizens of a certain amount of their income in order to fund journalism, how do we know what those people would have spent the money on had they been able to decide for themselves?" He added: "Who is to decide what quality journalism is, anyway? In a way, it should be the consumer, based on his or her need for information. Should it be left up to a roomful of bureaucrats to establish a collective standard of quality information?"

The argument about not using any tax dollars for public broadcasting is one that libertarians have lost, time and time again. Enough citizens have communicated their appreciation for public broadcasting that even a sufficient number of Republicans have refused to pull the plug on it.

And this idea that a "roomful of bureaucrats"—a typical straw man of libertarians—will be setting a "collective" (another boogeyman) standard is not what's being proposed. Instead, media scholars like McChesney and Pickard want citizens to be given vouchers to support the independent media outlet of their choice.

McChesney, in an email to me, added the following:

The profit-driven commercial news model based on advertising revenues only took off in the second half of the nineteenth century, and with the Internet that model is dead today, and no one is going to make profits investing in popular journalism again. That is why much of the nation is now a "news desert"—an unthinkable term just three decades ago—where there are no newsrooms with paid editors and reporters covering the communities. To continue the analogy, in terms of resources the USA has gone from the Amazon rain forest to the Sahara desert in the past three decades. No one in the business community thinks they can make a dime in journalism, and the current economic collapse of 2020 may eliminate the few remaining paid journalism jobs that remain. The Libertarian crowd and the Koch crowd have no problem with the elimination of journalism. It makes the control of society by those with the most property much more secure.

Politically, This Is a Hard Sell

Given the knee-jerk arguments against subsidizing independent journalism, getting this reform passed is not going to be easy. Hell, we can't even get public funding for universal health care in this country, so how are we going to get public funding for journalism?

But many of the proposals in this book are hard sells. All will take work. That doesn't invalidate their merits. And millions of citizens are already being organized by such groups as Free Press to demand media reform.

And actually, government funding for media may not be as hard a sell as you might think.

During the coronavirus pandemic, for instance, seventy-four US senators signed a letter urging the Office of Management and Budget to instruct federal agencies to support the media with increased advertising.

"Local newspapers and broadcasters have been particularly hit hard financially due to decreased revenue typically derived from advertising sales," said the letter, dated April 23, 2020. "We believe there is an opportunity for the federal government to provide relief to our local newspapers and broadcasters."

The senators wrote that this would serve a "vital, dual interest." They explained: "Increasing local advertising will both help disseminate important information to communities and support local media with revenue that will help keep them operating."

Anyway, who knows which comes first, universal health care or amending the Constitution to overturn *Citizens United* or getting massive funding for independent journalism? No one has a clear crystal ball. I know mine's foggy!

It's quite possible that many of the prodemocracy reforms that seem like a hard sell today will arrive in a rush. At some point, enough citizens are going to get so fed up with a system that promises them democracy—that promises them an equal voice—but fails miserably, time after time, to deliver on that promise that they will demand nothing short of a real democracy. We're very close to that point today.

Part II

chapter 11

Root Out Racism

The grotesque murder of George Floyd by Minneapolis police on May 25, 2020, reawakened much of America—and much of Wisconsin—to the racism that so pervades our society.

Racism is a fundamental evil, in and of itself, and must be eradicated. Racism is totally incompatible with democracy. A democracy is where everyone has an equal voice, and racism deprives people of color of their voice— and far too often of their breath too.

We've had our own George Floyds right here in Wisconsin.

So it was with the police killing of Larry Jenkins in Milwaukee on September 19, 2002.

So it was with the police killing of Justin Fields in Milwaukee on March 2, 2003.

So it was with the police killing of Tony Bean in Milwaukee on August 15, 2010.

So it was with the police killing of James Perry in Milwaukee on September 13, 2010.

So it was with the police killing of Derek Williams in Milwaukee on July 6, 2011.

So it was with the police killing of Dontre Hamilton in Milwaukee on April 30, 2014.

So it was with the police killing of Tony Robinson in Madison on March 6, 2015.

So it was with the police killing of Jay Anderson Jr. in Wauwatosa on June 23, 2016.

So it was with the police killing of Sylville Smith in Milwaukee on August 13, 2016.

So it was with the police killing of Adam Trammell in Milwaukee on May 25, 2017.

So it was with the police killing of Terry Williams in Milwaukee on June 11, 2017.

So it was with the police killing of Ty Rese West in Mt. Pleasant on June 14, 2019.

So it was with the police killing of Alvin Cole in Wauwatosa on February 2, 2020.

So it was with the police killing of Joel Acevedo in Milwaukee on April 19, 2020.

Most of these murders at the hands of police sparked local protests. But the George Floyd murder in Minnesota saw Black Lives Matter protests spring up all across Wisconsin, and they were overwhelmingly nonviolent. Here's a partial list:

Appleton	La Crosse	Rhinelander
Arbor Vitae	Lake Mills	River Falls
Ashland	Madison	Shawano
Barron	Manitowoc	Sheboygan
Bayfield	Marinette	Shorewood
Beaver Dam	Marshfield	Sister Bay
Beloit	Menomonee Falls	Stevens Point
Brookfield	Menomonie	Sturgeon Bay
Burlington	Mequon	Sun Prairie
Cedarburg	Merrill	Superior
Chilton	Milwaukee	Tomah
De Pere	Minocqua	Verona
Dodgeville	Monroe	Viroqua
Eau Claire	New Richmond	Washburn
Fond du Lac	Oconomowoc	Waterford
Franklin	Oconto	Waukesha
Grafton	Oshkosh	Waupaca
Green Bay	Plymouth	Wausau
Hayward	Port Washington	Wauwatosa
Hudson	Poynette	West Allis
Janesville	Prairie du Sac	West Bend
Kansasville	Racine	Whitefish Bay
Kenosha	Red Cliff	Wisconsin Rapids
Kewaunee	Reedsburg	

A Marquette University Law School poll on June 24, 2020, revealed that 61 percent of Wisconsinites supported these protests, including 59 percent of whites. This was a hopeful sign that Wisconsin might finally be ready to reckon with the vast and chronic racial disparities that have placed our state at the very bottom of so many rankings.

Then, on August 23, the issue of police brutality came home once again to Wisconsin when a white Kenosha police officer shot Jacob Blake several times in the back as he was trying to get into his car. The shooting, captured on video, reignited national outrage and sparked large protests in Kenosha. In the nights that followed, several buildings were burned down and some stores were looted. Governor Tony Evers called out the National Guard.

On August 25, Kyle Rittenhouse, a seventeen-year-old white kid from Antioch, Illinois, was driven up to Kenosha by his mother. He was armed with an AR-15 and was hanging out with other heavily armed white men who claimed they were protecting property. Police gave Rittenhouse some water, and told him and the other armed men, "We appreciate you guys. We really do."

A short time later, video showed Rittenhouse shooting Joseph Rosenbaum and Anthony Huber, both of whom died, and wounding one other. After shooting them, Rittenhouse walked with his hands up past several police vehicles. Bystanders yelled, "He just shot someone." But the police did not arrest him at the scene and let him return home. He is facing one count of first-degree intentional homicide and one count of attempted homicide.

The disparate treatment that Rittenhouse and Blake received at the hands of the police placed into sharp relief the issue of systemic racism. And comments by Kenosha County sheriff David Beth in 2018 highlight the individual racism that infects policing in Wisconsin. At a press conference about a couple of Black shoplifters at a Tommy Hilfiger store, Sheriff Beth went off:

> At least some of these males are going out and getting ten other women pregnant and having small children. Let's put them away. At some point, we have to stop being politically correct. And I don't care what race they are, I don't care how old they are. If there's a threshold that they cross . . . we put them away. We put them away for the rest of their lives so that the rest of us can be better. . . . These people are no longer an asset to our community and they just need to disappear. . . . We have to get rid of this group of people.

One month after the shooting of Blake, the *Washington Post* on September 20 ran an article documenting the racism in the Kenosha police department. "In dozens of interviews, Kenosha residents, community activists, former officials, and six current and former Kenosha police officers described a police culture bereft of diversity, tolerant of excessive force and determined to cover up for its own," the article said. "Of more than 200 officers on the force, only eight are Black, police officials acknowledged, and a Black person has never risen to the ranks of police chief, assistant chief or police inspector."

Jacob Blake's shooting and the history of police violence against Black males in Wisconsin are just the ugly backdrop on the reality of Black oppression in our state.

For years, article after article, study after study, report after report have cited Wisconsin as the rock bottom place to live if you're African American:

- "The Worst Place in the U.S. to Be Black Is . . . Wisconsin," *Dollars & Sense*, December 2015.
- "The Worst Place to Be Black in the U.S. Is . . . Wisconsin," *Boston Review*, October 29, 2018.
- "Report: Milwaukee, Racine Rank as Worst Cities for African Americans to Live," Wisconsin Public Radio, 2019.
- "Wisconsin Has Worst Racial Inequality, Report Says," WTMJ, February 7, 2020.
- "Wisconsin Is Most Segregated State in America, According to Report," channel3000.com, January 16, 2019.

Across the board, the disparities are glaring:

- A Black baby is three times more likely to die in infancy than a white baby in Wisconsin, as the Black infant mortality in Wisconsin is the worst in the nation.
- One of every three Black children in Wisconsin lives in poverty, a rate that is 3.5 times higher than that of white children. Wisconsin ranks fourth worst in the nation on this scale.
- "In Wisconsin, 14 percent of Black adults hold a Bachelors Degree while 30 percent of whites do. With whites more than twice as likely as Blacks to hold this level of education, Wisconsin posts the highest racial disparity in

the nation," according to "Race in the Heartland: Wisconsin's Extreme Racial Disparity," a report from the Center on Wisconsin Strategy (COWS).

Other statistics in that report include:

- Wisconsin has "the worst unemployment disparity in the country." In 2017, for instance, "black Wisconsinites were nearly three times more likely to be unemployed than white."
- "The median white household has annual income of just over $59,500 in Wisconsin. The median African American household annual income, $29,000, is a bit less than half the white level. Only two states post greater Black/white inequality in household income."
- "In Wisconsin, more than 70 percent of white families own their homes. At the same time, just 27 percent of Black families do. That difference is the eighth largest disparity in home ownership rates by race in the nation."
- "Black Wisconsinites are more than 11 times more likely to be incarcerated than are their white neighbors. Only in New Jersey is incarceration disparity more extreme."

The roots of racism in Wisconsin, as in America, run deep.

"Some of the first African Americans in Wisconsin were slaves," according to "Black History in Wisconsin," an essay at the website of the Wisconsin Historical Society (WHS). "In 1746, the commander of the French garrison at Green Bay brought a black slave with him. When the French surrendered Wisconsin to the English in 1760, the peace provisions allowed Charles de Langlade and other settlers to retain their 'negro and Pawnee' slaves."

Before Wisconsin became a state, "many of the white settlers who streamed into Wisconsin to mine lead in the 1820s and 1830s came from southern states and often brought slaves with them," the essay says, adding that some were freed and others were not.

Racism showed itself nakedly at Wisconsin's 1846 constitutional convention, where an amendment was proposed to strike the word "white" as a qualification for voting and thereby allow Black men to vote. This led to an ugly debate. A delegate named Mr. Ryan objected that Wisconsin would be "overrun with runaway slaves," according to a record of the proceedings at WHS titled "The Constitution of 1846." Ryan "believed God had placed an insuperable mark of separation upon the two races." And he disparaged

Black people in New York City, where "every Negro was a thief and every Negro woman far worse." He referred to Black people as "this unfortunate class of man," and said "it would be an injustice . . . to place the two races in the same scale of social equality."

Another delegate, Moses Strong, said he was "teetotally opposed to Negro suffrage in any manner of form than can be devised." He said: "If this Negro clause was inserted in the Constitution, it would not receive 50 votes west of the Rock River; the people would deem it an infringement upon their natural rights thus to place them upon an equality with the colored race." And he threatened "war to the knife, and the knife to the hilt" against the Abolitionist Party.

A few delegates argued strenuously in favor of it. A Mr. Gibson said, "The whole system of a republican government [was] opposed to depriving Negroes of the right to suffrage. The whole principle of republican institutions, from foundation to capstone, [was] opposed to infringing upon the natural rights of any man." As a result, he said, he "could not, therefore, vote for depriving this portion of citizens of their right to voting."

Another delegate, Mr. Manahan, said he "could not vote for depriving men of their suffrage unless relieved from taxation." Manahan added tartly that he "had always heard and believed that taxation and representation should go together."

The amendment to give Black men the right to vote failed.

Abolitionist sentiment grew in Wisconsin in the next decade. An abolitionist leaflet from 1854 for a mass meeting in Milwaukee gave out a clarion call:

Freemen of Wisconsin! In the spirit of our Revolutionary Fathers, come to this gathering of the Free, resolved to speak and act as men worthy of Free Heritage. Let the plough stand still in the furrow, and the door of the workshop be closed, while you hasten to the rescue of your country. Let the merchant forsake his Counting Room, the lawyer his brief, and the Minister of God his study and come up to discuss with us the broad principles of Liberty. Come then, one and all, form every town and village, come, and unite with us in the sacred cause of Liberty. Now is the time to strike for Freedom. Come, while the free spirit still burns in your bosom.

That same year, abolitionists freed Joshua Glover. "An escaped slave, Glover was captured and locked in a Milwaukee jail in 1854," notes the WHS essay. "A sympathetic mob broke Glover out and helped him to freedom. The mob's ringleader was arrested for breaking the law, but when he carried his case to the Wisconsin Supreme Court, justices declared the federal Fugitive Slave Law unconstitutional." Lest you indulge in a romanticized version of Wisconsin history, remember this: seven years later, a different kind of a mob in Milwaukee dragged a Black man named George Clark out of a Milwaukee jail and lynched him.

When the Civil War started, Wisconsin had only about 1,200 Black residents, and blatant racism prevailed. "Despite strong statewide support for the Union cause, most Wisconsin residents were not sympathetic to the plight of African Americans," the essay notes. "In 1863, petitions to outlaw further Black immigration into Wisconsin were introduced into the state Assembly several times. Segregation motivated by racial prejudice was supported both by mainstream public opinion and by Wisconsin's laws."

Black men in Wisconsin didn't win the right to vote until 1866. That year, "Ezekiel Gillespie, a leader in Milwaukee's Black community, sued for the right to vote and carried his case to the Wisconsin Supreme Court," where he prevailed, the essay notes.

But Wisconsinites continued to discriminate against Black people. "Following the Civil War, Wisconsin's white residents fought to limit the number of African Americans in this state and legalized segregation, socially and politically," says a report on the Wisconsin Department of Health Service's website titled "African Americans in Wisconsin: History."

The Black population in Wisconsin exploded in the twentieth century. In 1910, only about 3,000 African Americans were living in Wisconsin; by 1960, there were about 75,000, mostly in Milwaukee, lured here by decent jobs in the manufacturing sector.

But employers were often racist. Fred Lins, president of Lins-Hess Sausage and a member of the Social Development Commission of Milwaukee, said in 1963: "The Negroes look so much alike that you can't identify the ones that committed the crime," he said. "An awful mess of them have an IQ of nothing."

Enforced segregation in education and housing, discrimination in employment and lending, and police brutality sparked massive and sustained protests in Milwaukee in the 1960s, led by Lloyd Barbee, Vel Phillips, the NAACP's Youth Council and Commandos, and Father Groppi, among many others. This story is well told by Patrick D. Jones in *The Selma of the*

North: Civil Rights Insurgency in Milwaukee (2009). He shows the support that George Wallace had in Milwaukee when he ran for president in 1964, garnering 31 percent of the vote there. He reveals how active the Ku Klux Klan was. He tells how the Milwaukee NAACP office was firebombed on August 9, 1966. And he recounts two illustrative incidents of civil rights activists facing off against virulently racist white mobs.

"On Sunday evening, August 28, 1966, Father Groppi and members of the NAACP Youth Council led a procession of 150 civil rights supporters on a six-mile trek from their inner core Freedom House, on poverty-stricken North Fifth Street, to the tree-lined comfort of suburban Wauwatosa," he writes. They were going to picket in front of Judge Robert Cannon's house because he refused to resign from the Eagle's Club, which had a "whites only" policy. According to Jones, white onlookers "shouted obscenities, such as 'Go back to the zoo, nigger,' and, 'Nigger, go back to the jungle.' Some held signs reading, 'Groppi, Go Home,' 'Nigger Lover!' and 'Keep Tosa White.'"

A year later, on August 29, 1967, came the confrontation as civil rights activists crossed the Sixteenth Street Viaduct and entered the white South Side to demand an end to housing discrimination. "An effigy of a white priest, defaced with a swastika, swung by the neck from a rope," Jones writes. "The crowd leered at the passersby and hurled threats, jeers, and obscenities. Two of the counter-protesters held up a Confederate flag, while others waved signs that stated, 'White Power,' 'Bring Back Slavery,' 'Trained Nigger,' 'I Like Niggers: Everybody Should Own a Few.' Bottles, eggs, rocks, wood, firecrackers, urine, and spit began to fly. Shouts of 'Get yourself a nigger,' 'We want slaves,' 'E-I-E-I-E-I-O, Father Groppi's got to go,' and 'Kill . . . kill . . . kill . . . kill' could be heard." Then the mob became violent and "swarmed over marchers, newsmen, and officers. Rampaging whites beat huddled and fleeing civil right supporters—many of them children and women." Shortly after they returned to Freedom House, the civil rights activists had to flee because it had been lit on fire.

The ugliness, intimidation, and violence didn't deter the civil rights activists, though. For two hundred consecutive nights, they marched for open housing, eventually prevailing on the Common Council to pass an ordinance prohibiting housing discrimination.

But the success of the protests was partial and short lived, as racism remained intransigent and as economic changes—particularly, deindustrialization—had a devastating effect on the Black community in Milwaukee.

"Milwaukee's industrial base experienced a precipitous decline" in the last three decades of the twentieth century and the first decade of the twenty-first, notes the *Encyclopedia of Milwaukee*. "In 1970, nearly 74% of the Black men in the city were employed. By 2009 only 46.7% of Black men were employed."

This crisis was not contained to Milwaukee. "Thirty years ago, the state generated much better economic outcomes for Blacks who, on average, did better in Wisconsin than the national average," notes a report from COWS titled "Race in the Heartland: Wisconsin's Extreme Racial Disparity." "But across the last 40 years, opportunity and outcomes for Black residents in the state have fallen below national averages and the racial divide has grown."

Some biases are embedded in commercial institutions. Jim O'Keefe, director of the Madison Community Development Division, told WKOW in 2016 that "between 2006 and 2016, applicants of color were denied by mortgage lenders three times more frequently than white homebuyers" with the same qualifications.

As we've seen, the roots of racism against Black Wisconsinites are a tangle of personal prejudice by whites, cultural racism, institutional racism, and capitalism. (For more information, please visit the spectacular Wisconsin Black Historical Society/Museum at 2620 West Center Street, Milwaukee.)

A similar tangle has marred the experience of Native Americans, Latinos, Hmong, and other Asian Americans in Wisconsin.

Native peoples inhabited what is now Wisconsin for at least ten thousand years before white settlers arrived.

"In the summer of 1634, the Ho-Chunk, Menominee, and Potawatomi near present-day Green Bay awoke to a strange sight: a light-skinned visitor who arrived at their villages by canoe, bearing gifts and displaying metal objects the Ho-Chunk later described as 'thunder sticks.' The visitor was Jean Nicolet, a French trader. . . . Nicolet's 'thunder sticks' were, of course, firearms, and their introduction into Native culture would forever change the Indian nations," writes Patty Loew in her indispensable *Indian Nations of Wisconsin: Histories of Endurance and Renewal* (2013).

Europeans also brought disease, alcohol, and Christianity, all of which disrupted Native cultures. "Disease, warfare, and chaotic change in the late seventeenth century made tribal members vulnerable to Christian promises of salvation and deliverance from sorrow," Loew writes.

Gradually, British traders moved into the Great Lakes region, and their clash with the French led to the French and Indian War, where the British prevailed. According to Loew, during the Revolutionary War, as well as the War of 1812, "most of the Wisconsin tribes fought on the side of the British, not the Americans."

In the nineteenth century, the US government coerced Wisconsin's Indian tribes into signing treaties ceding their land. As a result, they lost tremendous wealth. UW–Stevens Point historian David Wrone estimated that the treaties with just the Chippewa in Wisconsin resulted in them losing 150 billion tons of iron ore, 100 billion board feet of timber, 13.5 billion pounds of copper, and 19 million acres of land to non-Natives.

Many Native American children were sent to government boarding schools, where they were discouraged "from speaking their Native language and expressing traditional culture," Loew writes. Kids as young as six went to the schools and were "prevented from returning home until after they graduated from high school."

Racism against members of Wisconsin's Indian tribes has been common-place since the founding of the state. And blatant racism against Native Americans came to a head in 1989 in what became known as the Walleye War. After US district judge Barbara Crabb in the 1987 *Voigt* decision affirmed the rights of the Ojibwe in Wisconsin to hunt and fish on their ceded lands, some white sports fishermen got up in arms that their walleye catch might go down. By the spearing season in 1989, they were intimidating the Ojibwe who were spearfishing. A white mob threw rocks and bottles and hurled disgusting words at them. A sign said, "Spare a walleye, spear a squaw." An Eagle River bar had the sign "Spear this!" next to a picture of a loaded gun.

Native Americans in Wisconsin fare far worse than white people across many indicators.

According to "Closing Gaps in Native American Health" by Kids Forward, "39.1% of Native American children live in poverty compared to 11.7% of their white counterparts. Additionally, just over half the native children in Wisconsin live in households where neither parent has full-time, year-round employment, while around one-fifth of white children face the same circumstance. These disparities exist because Native American communities often lack general resources, educational opportunities, and access to family-supporting jobs."

Native Americans are also far worse off when it comes to health. "From 2012–2014, infant mortality rates for native children in Wisconsin were 69% higher than those of white children," the report notes. "The 2014 age-adjusted mortality rate was nearly 50% higher for Native Americans in Wisconsin than for whites. . . . The 2014 average age at death for Native Americans was 63 years compared to 77 years for whites."

Native Americans in Wisconsin have also had their own problems with police. Nationally, they are killed by police at a higher rate than any other racial group, according to data from the Centers for Disease Control and Prevention. On November 8, 2017, on the Bad River Reservation, an Ashland police officer shot and killed fourteen-year-old Jason Pero, an event that led to outrage and protests there.

Over the past four decades, Wisconsin's Indian tribes have rallied to fend off threats to the environment from the US government and huge corporations. I was lucky enough to meet Walt Bresette, the great Red Cliff activist, who did so much to bring together Wisconsin tribal activists and environmentalists and engage everyone in creative nonviolent action. I also was fortunate to get to know Ada Deer, the Menominee activist, congressional candidate, and then assistant secretary of the interior, who has never given up the fight. And I admired the way Mike Wiggins, chairman of the Bad River Tribe, resisted the change in the mining law under governor Scott Walker and stressed how crucial the land and the water of Wisconsin are for his people and all people.

In the 1980s, the Menominee faced the possibility that the US Department of Energy was going to dump high-level radioactive waste on its ancestral lands in the Wolf River watershed, Loew notes. Menominee tribal chair Gordon Dickie led the opposition to the dump. "When DOE representatives came to Menominee High School for a public hearing, elders . . . and Menominee environmentalists 'chased them out of the meeting,'" Dickie's daughter, Rebecca Alegria, told Loew.

In the following decade, Exxon applied for permits to open the Crandon mine to get at 55 million tons of copper and ore, Loew notes. "The Menominee led a coalition of environmental groups" that successfully blocked the mine.

In 2011, the Bad River Reservation helped organize strenuous opposition to a new mining bill that Walker and the Republican-dominated legislature were trying to push through on behalf of the Gogebic-Taconite Company. On December 13, 2011, the Bad River Tribal Council wrote a position paper opposing the mine, saying it was "no more than a Christmas gift to a single out of state investor who owns GTAC and wants to weaken Wisconsin's mining and environmental laws to make huge profits for himself at the expense of Wisconsin citizens and Native Americans." The bill eventually passed, but GTAC did not go through with its mine. Resistance paid off again.

Latinos have been in Wisconsin since before statehood, but their numbers didn't rise significantly here "until the 1950s," according to "20th-Century Immigration," an article on the WHS website. "Prior to the 1950s, most Mexicans in Wisconsin were migrant laborers recruited by manufacturers and agricultural contractors to fill labor shortages caused by immigration laws that restricted the number of Europeans allowed to immigrate, as well as shortages caused by labor strikes. By 1925, around 9,000 Mexican Americans lived in Milwaukee but most lost their jobs during the Depression and moved back home."

In the last half of the twentieth century and the first two decades of the twenty-first, the Latino population in Wisconsin has continued to grow. Throughout, Latinos have had to contend with racism.

"Before civil rights laws passed, racism and discrimination were common for Hispanic/Latino families, making it difficult for them to obtain the necessities of daily life," says a Department of Health Services report titled "Hispanics/Latinos in Wisconsin: History."

Racism and discrimination didn't go away after the passage of civil rights laws.

In 1967, Carmen de la Paz, who later worked for decades for La Casa de Esperanza, moved to Waukesha with her husband. "When I came to Waukesha, we moved into an apartment," she recalls in *Somos Latinas: Voices of Wisconsin Latina Activists*. "I remember that the manager of a four-unit apartment told us that the other three neighbors, when they were told that he was renting to a Puerto Rican family, were against it. They told the manager that if he rented to us, they would move." She faced a similar experience when she and her husband bought a house a couple of years later. And her son was not treated well in the Waukesha public schools.

"When he started first grade, that was hell for him! He came home crying every day," she recalls. "He didn't want to go to school because the children pushed him and spit at him because of his color."

Sylvia Garcia, who helped create the Chicano and Latino Studies Program at UW–Madison, recalls going to the Brookfield mall in the late 1960s. "I remember two white guys going to their car and one of them actually called my mom 'Aunt Jemima.' I was so angry that I actually went over to their car and kicked it."

In a 1971 report, "Governor's Investigating Committee on Problems of Wisconsin's Spanish Speaking Communities," Latino community members drew special attention to "police racism" and "police insensitivity." They said: "The conduct of too many policemen assigned to the Latin American communities has long been a matter of concern."

They cited the case of "an elderly Puerto Rican gentlemen allegedly beaten by two policemen, later dying of internal injuries, for the offense of carrying his laundry across a yard."

They also mentioned "Latin leaders being followed by the police, stopped and held spread-eagle against their cars." And they noted "police provocation and violence upon the Latin people peacefully marching back from a protest."

By 2011, things weren't much better. "Milwaukee police pulled over Hispanic city motorists nearly five times as often as white drivers," according to a *Milwaukee Journal Sentinel* story on December 3, 2011.

Institutional racism against Latinos shows its face in economic statistics. "There is a deep disparity between the economic status of Latinx people in Wisconsin and that of Anglos," write Andrea-Teresa Arenas and Eloisa Gómez in *Somos Latinas*. "In 2014, the average annual income of Anglos was $31,400, that of African Americans was $21,000, and that of Latinx people was $20,000."

Then there's racism that Latinos face from whites on the street. On the evening of November 1, 2019, in Milwaukee, Mahud Villalaz, a US citizen who was born in Peru and has lived in Wisconsin for almost two decades, was about to enter a Mexican restaurant when a white man accosted him. His assailant yelled at him and accused him of being here illegally and claimed he was invading the United States. Then he threw acid on Villalaz's face, causing second-degree burns.

Confronting and combating racism, Latinos in Wisconsin have a rich activist history that I can only wave at here. In the 1960s, Ernesto Chacón, Jesús Salas, Avelardo Valdez, and others led rallies for Latino rights in Milwaukee. They organized a group called Obreros Unidos, which advocated for migrant workers in Wisconsin. Salas and David Giffey wrote about the organizing of migrant workers in their booklet "Struggle for Justice: The Migrant Farm Worker Labor Movement in Wisconsin," which was published by the Wisconsin Labor History Society in 1998.

"Twenty-four resolute marchers . . . left Wautoma, Wisconsin, in a light rainfall Monday morning, August 15, 1966," they write. "They headed west to Coloma, and then south along state Highway 51. After five days and eighty foot-sore miles, they presented their demands to state agencies at the Capitol in Madison. . . . The demands were basic:

- A $1.25 per hour minimum wage
- Improved housing
- Accident and hospitalization insurance
- A meeting with the Governor's Committee on Migratory Labor
- Public toilet facilities for use by farm workers in Wisconsin."

As Salvador Sanchez told the authors, "The animals in the stable would have better conditions than the humans in the field."

The following year, on August 23, 1967, "More than 400 adult workers and hundreds of children went on strike against Libby, McNeill & Libby, Inc. of Neshkora," Salas and Giffey write. In the next couple of years, there were walkouts in Cambria and in Hartford, they note.

And when César Chávez led the United Farm Workers into a national boycott of grapes and lettuce, there were "boycott actions in every major Wisconsin city," Salas and Giffey write. Latina activist Lupita Bejar Verbeten would often sing at these protests, according to *Somos Latinas*.

Latinos were also active in the labor movement in Milwaukee and Racine in the 1960s and 1970s. And in the early 1980s, the Latina Task Force was formed to advocate for women and their families. Other groups arose in the ensuing decades, such as Latinos United for Change and Advancement. Today, it is Christine Neumann-Ortiz of Voces de la Frontera, among others, who has shown tremendous skill in galvanizing the Latinx community over issues of ICE in Milwaukee, Dreamers, sanctuary cities, and driver's licenses for undocumented workers. JoCasta Zamarripa, first as a member of the state assembly and then as a Milwaukee alder, also stands out as a talented leader of the Latinx community in Wisconsin.

Asian Americans in Wisconsin make up the third largest racial group in the state, about 4.4 percent of the state's population, with Hmong comprising the biggest slice. In the 1980s and 1990s, as Hmong refugees began to settle first in Wausau and then in other predominantly white cities like La Crosse, Eau Claire, Green Bay, and Sheboygan, they were often met with outright racism. They were called "Chinks" and told to go back where they came from.

Linda Lawrence, who was mayor of Wausau from 1998 to 2004, told the *Chicago Tribune*: "People here weren't used to seeing people who weren't German or Polish. We've had 20 years of stormin' and normin' about who has the right to be here and what does it cost."

To this day, as with other people of color, Asian Americans in Wisconsin encounter racism in their day-to-day lives. It escalated during the coronavirus pandemic of 2020, when Donald Trump blamed China for it, calling it Kung Flu.

"The sharp rise in anti-Asian bigotry in the wake of the pandemic has been acutely felt in Wisconsin, where accounts of various forms of harassment have sown widespread fear and uncertainty within the Asian-American community," noted the ACLU of Wisconsin in a posting on its website on April 27, 2020. "A Chinese-Japanese restaurant in Milwaukee temporarily shut down after employees there encountered racist attacks. In Marathon County, home to a large and vibrant Asian-American community, people have faced verbal harassment and intimidation, with reports of individuals even being intentionally coughed on by other residents."

Several progressive nonprofit groups have organized to resist the anti-Asian sentiment, not least among them Freedom, Inc., in Madison and the Hmong American Women's Association in Milwaukee.

People of color in Wisconsin have to deal with racism at the personal, cultural, institutional, and structural levels. These are hurdles that white Wisconsinites don't have to clear, and that's the heart of the matter.

SOLUTIONS

Confront Racism Interpersonally

At the individual level, we can all do our part by challenging the racist statements that we may encounter in our social or occupational or familial settings. Too often, white folks let these slide, not wanting to make a scene, or taking the path of least resistance, or pretending to be "Wisconsin nice." But there's nothing "Wisconsin nice" about racism.

Support Racial Justice Organizations

Racial justice organizations are leading the way, and they need our support. Some of the best ones in Wisconsin are the African American Roundtable,

Black Leaders Organizing for Communities (BLOC), Freedom, Inc., Leaders Igniting Transformation (LIT), Urban Triage, and Voces de la Frontera.

Defund the Police

The calls to "Defund the Police" rang out loud and clear from protesters around the country after the George Floyd murder. The slogan can mean anything from abolishing the police to reducing their budget and reallocating some of the funds. The Movement for Black Lives says on its website, "When we talk about defunding the police, we're talking about making a major pivot in national priorities. We need to see a shift from massive spending on police that don't keep us safe to a massive investment in a shared vision of community safety that actually works." The Movement says, "Imagine alternatives to what violent policing might look like."

Michael Johnson, the leader of the Boys & Girls Club of Dane County, in an open letter to the Madison community on June 24, 2020, did just that. He proposed, among other things, to "repurpose $8.6M or 10% of MPD's budget to community policing, mental health services and community policing strategies to be managed by black-led organizations that are culturally competent, including grassroots groups and other communities of color."

State representatives Chris Taylor and LaTonya Johnson introduced a bill, AB 1012, in the last two sessions of the legislature on policing to improve practices. As summarized by the Legislative Reference Bureau, it would require that "the primary duty of all law enforcement is to preserve the life of all individuals; that deadly force is to be used only as the last resort; that officers should use skills and tactics that minimize the likelihood that force will become necessary; that, if officers must use physical force, it should be the least amount of force necessary to safely address the threat; and that law enforcement officers must take reasonable action to stop or prevent any unreasonable use of force by their colleagues." Governor Evers endorsed it in the wake of the George Floyd protests, but the bill went nowhere.

Former Madison police chief David Couper wrote, after the George Floyd murder, "Police are not solely responsible for the systemic inequalities in our society. But they must stop tolerating fellow cops who verbally and physically abuse others." That means the police union has to stop coddling these abusers too.

Pursue a Two-Generation Collaborative Strategy

Kids Forward in its 2014 policy brief "Race for Results: Wisconsin's Need to Reduce Racial Disparities" noted: "There are strategies for addressing disparities that we know can make a difference. Those include making sure that all families have meaningful paths to employment opportunities and family-supporting incomes; that their children have access to high-quality education, particularly early in life; and that communities are supported with the resources to pursue a two-generation approach that invests in both children and their parents." It listed some general principles that should guide the work to address racial disparities across Wisconsin:

1. We need to *authentically engage the families and communities most affected* by these disparities in identifying and implementing solutions.

2. Our approach needs to be *a two generation strategy*—one that supports under-resourced parents while intensifying investments in at-risk children, from cradle to career.

3. Our programs and services need to be woven together into a more integrated whole—one that is *comprehensive* and *collaborative*, not siloed.

4. Our major investments of money and time must be more effectively *targeted*, recognizing the greatest needs are heavily concentrated among low-income families of color.

5. The work ahead is not about placing blame, but about *accepting shared responsibility*.

6. Given the depth and breadth of our challenges, our responses have to be driven by *urgency* and sustained by *long-term commitment*.

Make It Easier to Own a Home or Start a Business

Owning a home or starting a business is a way for people of color to get a leg up. But coming up with the initial capital to do so is often prohibitive. That's why Michael Johnson has proposed the creation of a "$30 million endowment as a public/private partnership to help Black Madisonians start businesses in Dane County and to help purchase homes."

Pay Reparations

If we really want to root out racism and redress these racial economic disparities, we, as a nation, must offer reparations to the descendants of American slaves. As Nicole Hannah-Jones argued in a persuasive essay in the *New York Times Magazine* (June 30, 2020):

> Reparations are a societal obligation in a nation where our Constitution sanctioned slavery, Congress passed laws protecting it and our federal government initiated, condoned and practiced legal racial segregation and discrimination against black Americans until half a century ago. And so it is the federal government that pays. . . .
>
> The coronavirus pandemic has dispatched the familiar lament that even if it is the right thing to do, this nation simply cannot afford to make restitution to the 40 million descendants of American slavery. It took Congress just a matter of weeks to pass a $2.2 trillion stimulus bill to help families and businesses struggling from the Covid-19 shutdowns. When, then, will this nation pass a stimulus package to finally respond to the singularity of black suffering?

COUNTERARGUMENTS AND COMPLEXITIES

There Is No Systemic Racism in America

This isn't so much of a counterargument as it is a counterassertion. But it's an assertion that Trump administration officials at the highest levels made in the wake of the protests over the murder of George Floyd.

Here's Donald Trump's attorney general William Barr: "I think there's racism in the United States still but I don't think that the law enforcement system is systemically racist."

Here's Larry Kudlow, who was Trump's top economic adviser: "I don't believe there is systemic racism in the U.S."

Here's Trump's acting Homeland Security chief Chad Wolf: "I do not think that we have a systemic racism problem with law enforcement officers across this country."

Here's Trump's national security advisor Robert O'Brien: "No, I don't think there's systemic racism."

Repeated denials can't make systemic racism disappear within policing or the broader criminal justice system, as well as in education, health care, housing, lending, employment, and the culture at large, just to name a few areas.

Defund the Police Is Too Radical a Demand

When the Black Lives Matter protests started demanding "Defund the Police," some liberals quaked that it was too radical a demand, for a variety of reasons. Some said it was naive because it implied that we don't need police even for the most violent offenders. Some thought it was dismissive of the good cops that are on police forces. Some worried that it was just going to alienate more conservative white folks. But you know what? It worked! It forced changes in Los Angeles, Minneapolis, and New York City, among other places. And it posed two crucial questions: How can we reenvision policing, top to bottom, and how do we create a society where we need dramatically less policing?

Reparations Are a Nonstarter Politically

A June 2019 poll by Hill-HarrisX found that 56 percent opposed reparations while 20 percent favored them. A Gallup poll one month later showed reparations as even less popular, with 67 percent in opposition and 29 percent in favor. That's why some view reparations as a nonstarter politically. But polls can change. The murder of George Floyd at the hands of Minneapolis police awakened much of the country to the problem of racism in America. A June 2, 2020, poll from Monmouth University revealed a massive shift in views on racial injustice in America: "A majority of the public now agrees that the police are more likely to use excessive force with a black person than a white person in similar situations. Only one-third of the country held this opinion four years ago." The poll also found that "the number of people who consider racial and ethnic discrimination to be a big problem has increased from about half in 2015 to nearly 3 in 4 now." There may be a similar shift underway on the subject of reparations. And regardless of whether it's popular right now, part of being a decent political leader is to actually lead on an important issue, not follow.

Universal Programs Are Better Than Race-Based Ones

Some liberals and socialists believe that the most practical solution for rectifying racism in America is to enact universal programs that wouldn't be explicitly race-based but would have a tremendous positive impact on the lives of people of color. They reason that such programs would be an easier sell because they wouldn't risk inflaming racist sentiments in the white population. And so they advocate for universal health care, a living wage, more money for public education, college for free, economic assistance to the most impoverished communities—all of which would disproportionately aid communities of color.

But ultimately, this is a cowardly strategy, and it doesn't get at "the singularity of black suffering," as Hannah-Jones put it. We could enact all those programs, and still people of color would be victimized by racism. We need to name the problem head-on, and attack the problem head-on. The problem is white supremacy. There's no sense in dodging it.

chapter 12

Move toward Economic Democracy

There can be no real political democracy unless there is
something approaching economic democracy.

—TEDDY ROOSEVELT, 1914

We can have a democratic society or we can have the concentration of
great wealth in the hands of a few. We cannot have both.

—SUPREME COURT JUSTICE LOUIS BRANDEIS, 1941

I was arrested twice during the protests in the state capitol against governor
Scott Walker's attack on workers' rights.

The first time was intentional. It was November 1, 2011, and younger activists over the previous couple of weeks had been arrested in the Assembly
Parlor simply for holding signs or taking pictures. While it's legal in Wisconsin to carry a gun into the Assembly Parlor, it's not legal to carry a sign or a
cell phone, ridiculous as that is.

I wanted to support the activists who had already been arrested, so I and
some other older activists went up to the Assembly Parlor ourselves. I had
taped to my shirt a piece of paper that had the words of the First Amendment on it and the words of the Wisconsin Constitution that ensure the
rights to freedom of speech and assembly.

Sure enough, a couple of people with signs started to get arrested. And
then someone got arrested for taking a picture of them getting arrested.
And then I got arrested for taking a picture of the person taking a picture
of them getting arrested. It was all so absurd. And I wasn't even arrested by
a Capitol Police officer but by a young DNR warden, who was supernice
and seemed a bit embarrassed by the whole thing.

The second time I was arrested was unintended. It was August 15, 2013,
and I was there in my capacity as a journalist. (At the time, I was editor of
The Progressive magazine.) In the days before, the Capitol Police had begun
arresting protesters just for singing in the rotunda, which the Solidarity

Singers had been doing every day at noontime for two and a half years. I was interviewing elected officials and demonstrators before the arrests began, and then I saw police handcuff Bonnie Block, one of the Raging Grannies. I followed them as they took her down the hallway to the elevator and asked them what she had done wrong, whereupon one of the officers said, "Arrest him," and before I knew it, I was in handcuffs. They took me to the basement of the capitol with the other arrested protesters. One by one, all the demonstrators were released. But the cops didn't release me. They took me to the jail and booked me on "obstruction" and held me for about an hour and a half. They eventually dropped the charges, though the police report said I was threatening them with my pen.

The protests against Act 10 were a watershed moment for Wisconsin. Act 10 assailed the rights of public sector workers. It prohibited them from bargaining on working conditions and from seeking wage increases higher than the rate of inflation. It required them to pay a portion of their health insurance, which amounted to a 10 percent pay cut. And it required annual recertification of their unions by a vote of at least half the membership (not half of those voting, but half of the total members).

The enormous, spontaneous throngs that filled the streets of Madison in February and March 2011 held out hope, albeit briefly, that Act 10 would not go through, and that Walker's counterrevolution would be stopped in its tracks. Even though I had recently been diagnosed with lymphoma, it was thrilling to be at the protests, which were nonviolent and exhilarating, with people in creative costumes and waving clever homemade signs and chanting, "This is what democracy looks like!"

But the protests ultimately failed, and Act 10 went through. When he was running for reelection in 2014, Walker was asked whether he would sign a "right-to-work" law, which would assail the rights not of public sector workers this time but of private sector workers. Walker coyly demurred, saying, "It's not part of my agenda," and that it would never come to his desk. But it did come to his desk (as 2015 Wisconsin Act 1), and as soon as it landed there, he signed it.

As a result of Act 10 and the right-to-work law, Wisconsin's unionized workforce has plummeted from 14.2 percent in 2010 to 8.1 percent in 2019.

This is a disaster for economic equality in Wisconsin. Unions are one of the prime vehicles by which working people—union members and others alike—raise their standard of living. And unions are the only vehicle by which working people exercise any collective say over their conditions on the job. For a country that boasts so much about being a democracy, America is a place where most workers spend eight hours a day in a dictatorship.

Economic inequality is stark all across the country, and Wisconsin is no exception. "There is a vast gap between the incomes of the highest earners in Wisconsin and the incomes of typical Wisconsin residents," notes "Pulling Apart 2017," a study by the Center on Wisconsin Strategy and the Wisconsin Budget Project. "In Wisconsin, the top 1% of earners had income of $335,000 or higher in 2014. The top .01% in Wisconsin—the top 1 out of 10,000—had incomes of at least $6.5 million. In Wisconsin, the top 1% made, on average, 19 times the average annual income of $48,000 that the remaining 99% of residents made. . . . The average income of the top .01% in Wisconsin was 399 times the average income of the bottom 99% of Wisconsin residents."

This trend has been going on for decades. "Over the last 30 years, at a minimum, income inequality has been increasing," noted three UW–Madison community development specialists—Steven Duller, Tessa Conroy, and Matthew Kures—in a report they did in 2019 for WisContext.

Amazingly, those with the lowest incomes in Wisconsin are paying a higher percentage of their state and local taxes than the top 1 percent. Those in the lowest 20 percent pay, on average, 10.1 percent of their income in state and local taxes, whereas those in the top 1 percent pay 7.7 percent of their income, according to the Wisconsin Budget Project.

Viewed through a racial lens, Wisconsin is even worse. According to a June 2020 study by WalletHub, Wisconsin ranks fiftieth among the states on racial equality in terms of employment and wealth. The study compared figures across eight metrics for white and Black people in fifty states and the District of Columbia. Wisconsin ranked fiftieth (behind only the District of Columbia) on the median annual income gap and on the labor-force participation gap. Wisconsin also ranked fiftieth (behind only Maine) on the highest poverty gap between Black and white people.

This is not news. Reports called "Wisconsin's Extreme Racial Disparity" from COWS in 2013, 2017, and 2019 noted: "Relatively good outcomes for Wisconsin's white population and worse-than-national outcomes for the African American population create a large divide. Extreme disparities are evident across a broad range of indicators. The gap between outcomes for white and African American residents is not isolated to any one area. . . . Thirty years ago the state generated much better economic outcomes for

Blacks who, on average, did better in Wisconsin than the national average. But across the last 40 years, opportunity and outcomes for Black residents in the state have fallen below national averages and the racial divide has grown."

The landmark "Race for Equity" project of Kids Forward has highlighted these disparities, especially in Dane County. But the organization has also looked statewide. In 2014, it put out a paper titled "Race for Results: Wisconsin's Need to Reduce Racial Disparities," which noted: "Thirty percent of Wisconsin's white children live in households below 200% of the poverty level, while nearly 80% of African-American children experience that level of economic insecurity. Meanwhile, about two-thirds of Wisconsin's Latino and American Indian kids live in households below 200% of the poverty line."

At this point, we don't need more reports, studies, newspaper articles, or commissions to expose the problem of Wisconsin's economic disparities.

SOLUTIONS

Strengthen Unions

We need to repeal Act 10 and the right-to-work law. Unions raise the wages not only of their own members but of nonunion workers as well. They are also crucial for giving workers a voice. And unions have been instrumental in lifting the standards of living of Black people, who are in unionized jobs at a higher percentage than white workers.

Raise the Minimum Wage to $15 an Hour

The "Fight for $15" is one of the key battles for economic justice in Wisconsin and around the country. The minimum wage in Wisconsin has been at just $7.25 an hour since 2008. That is not a living wage. In fact, it's 29 percent less, in real terms, than the minimum wage fifty years ago, according to the Economic Policy Institute.

Expand the Earned Income Tax Credit

As the Wisconsin Budget Project notes, "The EITC has a proven track record of helping parents with low-wage jobs keep their heads above water and provide their children with better lives. Increasing Wisconsin's EITC would help counteract the increasing concentration of income and wealth in a few hands—hands that are most likely to be white, due to a long history of racial discrimination." Governor Tony Evers proposed boosting the earned income tax credit, but the Republican-dominated legislature threw out his plan.

Provide Free High-Quality Childcare

Senator Elizabeth Warren proposed free childcare in her run for the Democratic nomination in 2020. The exorbitant cost of childcare is hard on many working families, who often face harsh choices about where to leave their kids when they go to work. Providing free, high-quality childcare would be better for the kids, the parents, and their job options.

Increase Spending on Early and K–12 Public Education

Early education is the first rung on the ladder out of poverty. The State of Wisconsin should contribute to programs like Early Head Start and Head Start, which are crucial for children's development. And we need to expand funding for public education, which was savagely cut by Walker, to spread opportunity much more broadly.

Offer Free College Education

Bernie Sanders made this a central plank of his run for the Democratic nomination, knowing that the cost of a college education is prohibitive for many. "The average annual in-state college tuition in Wisconsin was $15,905 for the 2018–2019 academic year," according to Collegecalc. "This is $1,498 higher than the U.S. average." Technical college tuition runs about $4,000 in Wisconsin, and that makes a big dent too.

Make the State Income Tax More Progressive

Wisconsin has a relatively flat income tax. Those making the least amount of money pay a 3.86 percent rate, which even the right-wing MacIver Institute recognizes is "one of the highest bottom-most income tax rates in the country." Those making $258,950 or more pay 7.65 percent—less than twice what the poorest pay. And there are no increases once you make more—even a lot more—than $258,950. So someone who makes $50 million or $500 million in Wisconsin pays the same rate as someone making $260,000. That's not right. The state should also eliminate the 30 percent reduction on capital gains on nonfarm property held for more than a year. This is a giveaway to the investor class.

Impose an Estate Tax or a Wealth Tax

For almost all of the twentieth century, Wisconsin imposed an estate tax, but it no longer has one. And since the federal government exempts estates under $11.58 million, any Wisconsinite who dies with, say, $11 million can give it all to their heirs, tax free. This is one way the wealthy reproduce each other. Having an estate tax is the most painless way to fund government services, and Wisconsin should reinstitute one.

When she ran for president in 2019, Warren proposed a wealth tax on Americans with more than $50 million in assets, and 63 percent of the public supported it, including 57 percent of Republicans.

It's actually an old idea. Thomas Jefferson was in favor of a wealth tax as a way of, in his words, "silently lessening the inequality of property." He wrote that it was a good idea to "exempt all from taxation below a certain point, and tax the higher portions of property in geometrical progression as they rise." And get this: Donald Trump himself, back in 1999, proposed a one-time tax on people with more than $10 million, and that tax, he said, should be 14.25 percent.

So if it's good enough for Thomas Jefferson, Elizabeth Warren, and Donald Trump, it ought to be good enough for us.

Restore the Safety Net

According to the Wisconsin Poverty Project at UW–Madison, the safety net in Wisconsin has a lot of holes in it. "In past years, particularly during the Great Recession, the safety net provided an important buffer against poverty, but its effects have shrunk over time as fewer people apply for and receive benefits. Benefit changes such as work requirements for single people in Food-Share have also reduced the number of people eligible to receive assistance," the 2017 Poverty Report noted. "Work expenses (including child care) and medical out-of-pocket expenses" largely negated the positive impacts of some of the social safety net programs the state offers. If we're serious about confronting economic inequality, we've got to fix the holes in the safety net.

Provide Universal Basic Income

In his run for the Democratic nomination for president in 2020, Andrew Yang brought front and center the idea of a universal basic income for every American. He didn't invent the idea; it's been around for a while. George McGovern talked about in 1972, and socialist economists have been proposing it for decades. But it's become more relevant as technology has been taking away more and more jobs, as Yang never tired of mentioning. And when the coronavirus forced an economic shutdown, the idea that the government should send people enough money so they could at least survive took on added urgency.

Combat Racism across the Board

Wisconsin's abysmal record on racial economic disparities won't be solved just by implementing the reforms above. Nor will they be solved simply by better enforcement of nondiscrimination laws in housing, employment, and lending. Nor will they be solved by providing important criminal justice reforms. To really get at the roots of racial economic disparities, we need to combat racism across the board: interpersonally, structurally, institutionally.

Ensure Real Equality of Opportunity

Grotesque income and wealth inequality—in Wisconsin and across the country—gives the lie to our much ballyhooed belief in equality of opportunity.

It's a joke, and a bad one, to say that the children growing up in the poorest of families in America have the same opportunity to live as comfortably as the children of Bill and Melinda Gates.

And it's also a bad joke to say that the children of a single mom living in poverty have the same opportunity to get into a decent college as the children of two Ivy League professors.

An interesting thought experiment, à la the Harvard philosopher of justice John Rawls, is to consider how you would propose to distribute wealth or income or opportunity if you had no idea whatsoever what your situation at birth would be. I doubt you would countenance our current setup.

At a minimum, I suspect most people would be in favor of a floor of decency in Wisconsin, and across the country. That's what FDR called for in his tenth State of the Union address on January 11, 1944, when he proposed his "Economic Bill of Rights."

But we also need elevators to the top, where everyone has an equal opportunity to ride them. One of those elevators is early childhood education. Another is college. Another is a decent job at a living wage.

Imagine Economic Democracy

Teddy Roosevelt said we need something "approaching economic democracy." Well, what would that look like? It wouldn't be just a collection of reforms, like those I've outlined. It would also be a new way of self-governance.

Joel Rogers, the director of COWS, has given this some serious thought. In *The Nation* (March 23, 2015), he proposed "an alternative egalitarian and democratic project." He wrote: "We usually think of democracy as a source of inclusive representation and distributive fairness, which it surely is. But it is also a source of problem-solving, invention and thus wealth generation— a source of value, not just values." He calls this alternative system "productive democracy"—or PD, for short—and explains:

> Along with seeking economic security and opportunity for all, PD would highlight the centrality of fostering both social learning and productivity . . . in achieving more ambitious egalitarian ends. It would place a bigger and more visible bet than social democrats ever did on a well-ordered democracy's ability to help citizens create social wealth—and solve social problems. Its signature politics would be efforts to develop and harness that contribution. Indeed, it would define the "general welfare" not just as physical and economic security and reasonably equal opportunity and life chances, but as the capacity and interest of all citizens to make such contributions, to be actively engaged in building their own society.

I like that vision. That's what economic democracy could look like.

COUNTERARGUMENTS AND COMPLEXITIES
Let the Free Market Decide Everything

This is the libertarian argument, favored by Charles Koch and his ilk. But the idea of the free market is a myth: government has been helping out businesses since day one, whether by building roads, or providing police, or by using its influence overseas to expand markets, or by doing research and development on pharmaceuticals or the internet.

And beyond that, we as a democracy have recognized for more than a hundred years that businesses can't be left unregulated or they will trample on workers' rights and workers' safety, they will produce dangerous products, and they will pollute the environment. And so, through our elected officials, we abolished child labor, we established a minimum wage, we established the Food and Drug Administration, and we established the Environmental Protection Agency.

We've also recognized, as a democracy, that we need revenues to "provide for the common defense" and to "promote the general welfare." That's why we have taxes. As Oliver Wendell Holmes put it, "Taxes are what we pay for a civilized society."

The question is, how civilized are we going to be?

$15 an Hour Will Hurt Poor People

An article at forbes.com on July 10, 2019, by Jack Kelly summarized this counterargument well: "Raising the minimum wage has a number of serious and negative unintended consequences. Employers, especially small family and midsize businesses, will be disproportionately hurt by the extra costs incurred. The local neighborhood stores and businesses with razor-thin profits will be forced to raise prices to make up for the additional labor costs. With the increased prices, customers may elect to take their business elsewhere. Losing customers means losing income, which could result in the business having to lay off workers."

A few months earlier, Ben Zipperer, an economist with the liberal Economic Policy Institute, supported the increase of the minimum wage to $15 an hour by 2024 before the House Committee on Education and Labor. "The bulk of recent economic research on the minimum wage, as well as the best scholarship, establishes that prior increases have had little to no negative consequences and instead have meaningfully raised the pay of the low-wage workforce," he testified on February 7, 2019. "My colleague David Cooper has estimated that raising the minimum wage to $15 by 2024 would lift the pay of about 40 million workers, or 27 percent of the eligible workforce. Affected workers who work year-round would receive a raise on the order of $3,000 a year. This is enough to make a tremendous difference in the life of a preschool teacher, bank teller, or fast-food worker."

Zipperer, who has studied the effect of minimum wage rates across the country, discounts the fear-mongering that a minimum wage of $15 an hour would have a lot of negative consequences. "There has been little downside to raising minimum wages," he writes, even in places with the highest increases.

Most Americans Disapprove of the Estate Tax

Though most Americans have consistently favored increasing taxes on the rich for many years, for a long time they have also disapproved of the estate tax. As recently as March 2016, Americans wanted to eliminate the estate tax, 54 percent to 19 percent, according to a Gallup poll. But those numbers are going down. A Quinnipiac poll in May 2017 showed almost an even split, with 48 percent for eliminating the tax and 43 percent for keeping it. And when Bernie Sanders introduced legislation to reduce the exemption on estates down to $3.5 million in 2019, which you may have thought would be vastly unpopular, that wasn't the case at all: "Fifty percent of voters in a February 7–10 Morning Consult/Politico survey favor the proposal, while 29 percent oppose it," according to its 2019 poll. It looks like Americans have flipped on the estate tax.

Economic Democracy Is Pie in the Sky

Several proposals in this book may seem like pie in the sky to you, but that doesn't make them not worth fighting for. And sometimes you need to envision pie in the sky before you can bake it and taste it down here on your plate. That's what I like about Joel Rogers's sketch of "Productive Democracy." He's not content just to ameliorate some of the problems we face, by tinkering here and there. He forces us to reimagine the society we really want to live in. We don't engage in that exercise enough. None of us was around when the social compact was signed in 1776 or 1789. We didn't get a say in it. What if we took the time to imagine the society we really wanted to live in? What if we contemplated what a real democracy would look like, one where we all have an equal say and we all can participate as equals? Give me a slice of that pie in the sky!

Conclusion

Why I'm Hopeful

I recognize that democracy has been taking a beating lately, here in Wisconsin and nationally. But I don't lose heart, and I don't give up.

Here are a few reasons I remain hopeful.

First, I travel all over the state of Wisconsin and I see the amazing work that grassroots activists are doing every day.

Thanks to the hard work of organizers for Wisconsin United to Amend, 166 communities in Wisconsin have passed resolutions or referendums in favor of amending the US Constitution to proclaim, once and for all, that corporations aren't actually persons and money isn't speech. Because of this organizing effort, Wisconsin is second only to Massachusetts in the number of communities that have signed on to this effort to overturn *Citizens United* and the other Supreme Court decisions that are blocking our way forward on the campaign finance issue.

Another example is the growing movement in Wisconsin to ban gerrymandering. By the end of 2020, 54 of the 72 counties had passed resolutions urging the legislature to pass a law giving us nonpartisan, independent redistricting. And twenty-eight counties had passed referendums by overwhelming margins to do the same. Many of those counties are red, red counties, but people across the board want an end to the manipulation by those in power.

People in Wisconsin believe in fairness. They just want a level playing field. That shouldn't be too much to ask.

I'm also hopeful because of the Black Lives Matter movement and the tremendous amount of activism it has sparked all across our state. To see nonviolent protests in dozens of our communities in 2020—some that had never seen an antiracism protest before—was a balm to my spirit.

And I'm hopeful because, over the past five years, I've seen the progressive nonprofit sector in Wisconsin unify itself and work harmoniously toward our shared goals. We've torn down our silos and we've shelved our egos (for the most part!), and we've got a lot of young and impressive leaders taking on more and more responsibility. They will lead us forward.

I'm hopeful, too, because of the strong advocates in our legislature for prodemocracy reform. You met many of them in the preceding chapters.

And I'm hopeful because of the inspiring prodemocracy leaders we have on the national scene, such as Stacey Abrams, Alexandria Ocasio-Cortez, Bernie Sanders, and Elizabeth Warren.

I also take hope from the mass movement to combat the climate crisis, and the activism of young people in driving this movement.

Frankly, part of being hopeful is a state of mind. Here's the great Irish poet Seamus Heaney:

> Once in a lifetime
> The longed-for tidal wave
> Of justice can rise up,
> And hope and history rhyme.
> So hope for a great sea-change
> On the far side of revenge.
> Believe that further shore
> Is reachable from here.

I believe we can reach that shore, but I have to confess I don't take comfort in my least favorite Martin Luther King Jr. quote: "The arc of the moral universe is long but it bends toward justice." I don't believe that. History isn't an arc; it's a zigzag. It's a dizzying and sometimes horrifying ride, with stops at the Middle Passage and Auschwitz, the Belgian Congo, Hiroshima and Nagasaki, Indonesia in 1965, My Lai, the Nanjing Massacre, Pol Pot's Cambodia, Stalin's Russia, and Wounded Knee, to name just a few of the low points. And of course, there have been high points too: abolishing slavery, enacting universal suffrage, mass literacy, and a decline in absolute poverty worldwide, among others.

But history is not going in one direction. And it is not predetermined. We all, with concerted action, can affect its direction and outcome.

So I much prefer this quote from Ta-Nehisi Coates: "History is not solely in our hands. And still you are called to struggle, not because it assures you victory but because it assures you an honorable and sane life."

None of us is assured of victory, but I know one thing for certain: great democracy reforms won't happen without citizen activism and mass movements.

That's the lesson I learned from Ralph Nader, for whom I worked after I graduated from college. And that's the lesson I learned from the people's historian Howard Zinn, who wrote for me at *The Progressive* magazine in the last dozen years of his life.

On my wall at the Wisconsin Democracy Campaign is a quote from Zinn, which I pass out to folks who come to my talks:

> To be hopeful in bad times is not just foolishly romantic. It is based on the fact that human history is a history not only of cruelty, but also of compassion, sacrifice, courage, kindness. If we remember those times and places—and there are so many—where people have behaved magnificently, this gives us the energy to act, and at least the possibility of sending this spinning top of a world in a different direction. And if we do act, in however small a way, we don't have to wait for some grand utopian future.... To live now as we think human beings should live, in defiance of all that is bad around us, is itself a marvelous victory.

So let's defy all that is bad around us, and celebrate all that is good.

I hope my offerings in this book will help move Wisconsin forward, and I welcome any ideas you have to make real the promise of democracy in our state.

As Fighting Bob La Follette put it, "The cure for the ills of democracy is more democracy."

Let's take the cure!

Affirmations for Surviving
the New Dark Ages

These are remarks I delivered to the American Association of University Women, UW–Madison Chapter, on August 27, 2020.

Thanks for inviting me to speak at your Public Policy meeting again.

I'd be remiss if I didn't mention, right at the top, the crisis we're facing in this state, and in this country, when it comes to systemic racism.

We saw a horrific illustration of that systemic racism in the shooting of Jacob Blake in Kenosha on Sunday.

But it's not an isolated incident. Prior to this, we'd had a dozen George Floyds right here in Wisconsin over the last decade, with Dontre Hamilton and Tony Robinson being only the most prominent.

This has got to stop, as does the excusifying for the police.

We need new, strict policies on the use of lethal force, and we need to root out racism now.

We also need to do something about all those semiautomatic weapons on our streets, as we saw to our horror in Kenosha on Tuesday night.

We need to take a stand.

And I'm sure grateful for the courage and the leadership of the Milwaukee Bucks and the NBA. They're showing us all how to do it.

My friends, we're living in a difficult time.

It's a difficult time because we haven't come to terms with racism in America, even after four hundred years.

It's a difficult time because we're in the midst of barbaric capitalism, which is forcing people to work under lethal conditions or starve.

And it's a difficult time because, frankly, the Age of Enlightenment is over.

It's dead.

We're in a new Dark Ages, with superstition and tribalism in the ascendancy, joined dangerously now not just by quack conspiracies—I give you QAnon—but also by refried prejudices and resurgent nationalisms.

Plus, millions of Americans are suffering from nightly "truth decay," as they are being fed lies and distortions on propaganda channels like Fox News.

And we're all in our separate camps. In a sense, we're living in totally different intellectual universes, which makes it difficult to have a conversation with people from the other universe who are being fed vastly divergent explanations for what's going on in this country and in the world.

In these new Dark Ages, the very idea of "truth" is under assault, as Michiko Kakutani, the longtime book editor at the *New York Times*, wrote in her book *The Death of Truth*.

In such a circumstance, how do you differentiate between fake news and real facts? That's one of the trick questions you asked me to answer tonight.

Well, I'll give it a try.

1. Read broadly. Find the most respectable sources you can find. But read around.

2. Go to the primary source, not the mediated one. If you didn't see Pence's speech last night, google it. Watch it for yourself. Don't depend on the media stories about it.

3. Be skeptical of everything you read and consume. Be even skeptical of your own ideas and beliefs. As the German philosopher Jürgen Habermas once said, reserve 10 percent of your brain for self-doubt.

4. Scrutinize everything. If something seems too facile in your own belief system or argument, fact-check it yourself!

5. Don't just read the headlines, especially on Facebook! We're all busy but we've got to get past just reading the headlines and clicking "like" or "share" even without reading the article. I've done it myself. I've shared something on Facebook only to realize later that it's a two-year-old story. That's embarrassing. We can't be lazy like that.

So these are some of the ways to distinguish real facts from "alternative facts," as Kellyanne Conway once notoriously put it.

I'm sure you're already an informed voter.

And as an informed voter, I hope you're able to discern the truth about absentee or mail-in voting. Because the truth of the matter is, it's tried and true. It's safe and secure.

Members of our armed services have been doing mail-in voting for decades—with no problems.

Five states, including Utah, do entirely mail-in voting—with no problems.

And fraud is not a problem because states safeguard mail-in ballots by using signature verification, tracking barcodes, twenty-four-hour surveilling of ballot drop-boxes, and setting clear chains of custody for all ballots.

Now, of course, given the slowdown at the post office, you should get your absentee ballot in early, or drop it off at your clerk's office yourself if it's getting close to Election Day.

I'm sure you don't need my encouragement, but by all means vote. Your website itself noted how important this election is.

If you want to tell your friends where to go to get information about voting, they can go to myvote.wi.gov.

Or they can go to the League of Women Voters of Wisconsin's website at my.lwv.org/Wisconsin.

I know you're going to be hearing from their executive director, Deb Cronmiller, soon, but let me give them a plug. I love the league! They have on their website a section called "Voter Information," which tells you not only how to register and what documents you need to vote, but also how to gather information on candidates so you can make an informed choice. It also publishes an issue guide on candidates for office, so you can see where they stand on many issues that might be important to you. And you can always go to a candidate's website and compare that candidate's position with those of the candidate's opponent.

You can also go to our website, www.wisdc.org, to see who's funding them. Click on "Follow the Money," then "Look Up Candidates," and then click on "Campaign 2020." We also have info on some of the outside groups that are splattering our screens with mud, so go to "Follow the Money" on our site, click on "Track Dark Money," and then click on "Hijacking Campaign, 2020."

So that's how you can educate yourself as a voter.

Figuring out how to educate other voters can be tough, frankly, depending on who they are.

If they're open to rational conversation but just don't know about the candidates, especially in down-ballot races, you can give them the info you have or steer them to the League of Women Voters or forward them articles you see in the local papers on those races.

And down-ballot races are vitally important, as we've learned here in Wisconsin over the last decade.

It really matters who is governor.

It really matters who has control of the legislature, and whether there is a veto-proof majority or not.

It really matters who is on the state supreme court.

It really matters who is your mayor, and who is on your city council.

It really matters who is your county executive, and who is on the county board.

And yes, it really matters who your sheriff is. Just look at Kenosha.

In this Age of COVID-19, for some, who your local officials are has actually been a matter of life and death.

So yes, encourage everyone you know to vote—and to vote down-ballot.

But if people are dug in ideologically, it's hard to know where to start.

Here's an example.

I play poker, Texas Hold'em, and some of the other players, let's just say, don't see the world the way I do.

After the shooting of Jacob Blake, one of them posted on Facebook the rap sheet on Jacob Blake, and sneered at those of us who were protesting. My approach, always, is to be polite and try to engage. So I said, "C'mon man! Just because he had a rap sheet doesn't justify the cops shooting him seven times in the back or justify the mocking of those of us who oppose racism and police brutality. You're better than that, my friend!"

Not sure it made a difference. He didn't respond. But I do have a relationship with him. In fact, just a few weeks ago, he posted something about lamenting the Facebook Friends he has lost because of his posts, and I responded that it wasn't worth losing friends over posts. So we'll see how that goes.

Here's another example. A few houses down from where I live, the neighbors are flying two big "Trump 2020" flags. I don't know these neighbors. I have had only one conversation with them, while my wife and I were out walking, which was pleasant enough. It was mostly about birds because they've got, like, ten bird feeders out, and I'm a big birder myself. So if I were on Team Biden, I might send them some information on Trump and his attempt to gut the Migratory Bird Treaty, but I'm not sure it'd make a dent.

Because I think we're actually fooling ourselves when we believe that if we only give voters the right article, the perfect leaflet, the most coherent argument, the cleverest meme, or the most informative website, they'll come around to our way of thinking.

Unfortunately, it doesn't work that way. There've been a lot of studies showing that people will repel the fact that disproves their beliefs rather than change their beliefs.

So I think educating voters is more of a long process of building relationships and engaging in conversation with people we know—first over shared values and only then on the particular issue that concerns you.

That's really our task, whether it's about racism or the unequal economy or climate change or any other crucial issue that concerns us and confronts our democracy.

So my advice is to work on people closest to you, those you're already in relationship with—family members, friends, people you socialize with.

And don't preach to them. Talk to them where they're at. Listen to and acknowledge their concerns. And try to nudge them along.

That's all I do these days: nudge, nudge, nudge.

And if we all nudge, nudge, nudge the people closest to us, we may be able to survive the New Dark Ages.

As W. H. Auden said, eighty-one years ago, "All I have is a voice to undo the folded lie."

And he ended his "September 1939" poem this way: "May we, beleaguered by the same negation and despair, show an affirming flame."

And what do we affirm?

Let's affirm the Enlightenment.

Let's affirm facts.

Let's affirm science.

But let's also affirm values, such as solidarity, racial equity, democracy, freedom, equality, and justice.

And let's also affirm love and kindness and friendship and working together for a full democracy, where everyone has an equal voice.

May these affirmations prevail!

On Respectful Dialogue

This is the text of the talk I gave to the League of Women Voters of Ripon on February 8, 2018.

I'd like to thank the League of Women Voters of Ripon for inviting me here tonight, and I'd like to thank everyone for coming.

I love the League of Women Voters! You do amazing work at the grassroots for our democracy here in Wisconsin, and I've spoken to many of your local chapters—from Ashland to Sturgeon Bay, from La Crosse all the way down to Whitewater and points in between.

Your members are key players in our democracy. You do the work locally, and that's the most important place to do it. It's better than coming to Madison to protest or Washington, DC. Because you can interact with your neighbors and colleagues, with the people you worship with and exercise with. They know you, and if they like you and respect you as a person, they are more likely to consider your views, even if they don't agree with you on them. And that's how political change begins.

I feel strongly about the need for respectful political dialogue across our differences.

I believe in discussion.

I believe in debate.

I believe in the fair exchange of ideas.

I'm an old John Stuart Mill guy: I believe the truth will ultimately prevail.

It's important, in this day and age especially, that we're able to converse, respectfully, with people who don't agree with us.

And that's what I try to do.

If you've heard me on Wisconsin Public Radio on their *Friday Week in Review* show, you know that I try to carry on a political debate respectfully.

I don't call my conservative counterpart names.

I don't belittle him or her.

I try to score points by being better prepared, faster on my feet, and by appealing not only to logic and facts, but to our highest values as Americans.

If it's just a food fight, I don't want any part of it.

So I search for places where we can have civil dialogue.

That's why I like WPR.

That's why I like writing op-eds for newspapers like the *Journal Sentinel* or the *State Journal*.

There are just too few places these days where you can engage in respectful political dialogue and debate.

Too often, we're in our own worlds.

People on the right can watch *Fox and Friends* in the morning, listen to Rush Limbaugh during the day, and watch Hannity at night and then start all over again the next morning.

And if you're on the left, you can watch Amy Goodman on *Democracy Now!* in the morning, listen to Progressive Radio during the day, read *The Nation* when you get home, and watch Rachel Maddow on MSNBC at night and start all over again the next morning.

And if you live in Madison and work at the many progressive nonprofits there and live on the Isthmus, you might not run into anyone in a week's time who disagrees with you!

This is unhealthy.

It doesn't build empathy.

It doesn't build intellectual muscle.

And it's bad politics because the essence of politics is the effort to persuade your fellow citizens that your view of what is just and right and beautiful and fair is the way to go.

So if you're talking to only people like yourself, you're not getting the job done.

And you're not going to have a clue about how to persuade those who don't already agree with you.

Similarly, being rude or vulgar is bad politics.

You don't persuade anyone on the other side by yelling at them.

You don't persuade anyone on the other side by swearing at them.

You can look at my Facebook posts from the first day I joined, and I can assure you that you won't find me ever swearing at anyone, and I post a lot, and I often post when I'm upset about something. But I try to do it respectfully.

But this is where it gets tricky.

How do you define "disrespectful"?

I, for one, don't believe it's disrespectful to sit down during the State of the Union, for instance, and not to clap when the president wants you to clap.

And I certainly don't think that's treasonous behavior. For Trump to suggest that it is shows that he has no appreciation for our First Amendment whatsoever.

On the other hand, interrupting President Obama when he was giving the State of the Union speech by yelling out "Liar" I would say is disrespectful.

And it's not because I prefer Obama to Trump that I say that. It's that the traditional norms of political discourse don't include heckling the president if you're a member of Congress.

And as Obama liked to say, "We can disagree without being disagreeable."

That makes sense to me; that's how I like to roll too.

By "disrespectful," I tend to mean rude or vulgar.

This obviously is a subjective thing, and you might define "disrespectful" differently than I do. There's no hard and fast rule.

But let me make things trickier still.

My problem is that I am so disgusted by a lot of what I see Governor Walker and Majority Leader Fitzgerald and Speaker Vos doing that I feel the moral obligation to convey that in strong terms.

How do I do that without being disrespectful?

And I'm so disgusted and—frankly—petrified by what I see Donald Trump doing that I feel the moral obligation to convey that in the strongest possible terms. I'm scared that he's going to start a nuclear war. I'm scared that he's going to destroy our democracy.

How do I do that without being disrespectful?

And even more to the point, when is the compulsion to be "respectful" an abdication of my moral obligation to tell it like it is and to try to arouse my fellow citizens to the crisis at hand?

So how do I wrestle with this problem?

Well, I still don't swear—unless I'm on the tennis court or at the poker table.

And I'm still not personally rude.

For instance, if I see Speaker Vos or Majority Leader Fitzgerald, I don't scream at them. A couple weeks ago, I saw Vos in his car outside the capitol, and I waved. And a few days later, I saw Fitzgerald at the Tornado Club, the best steakhouse in Wisconsin, and I was standing just five feet away from him, and I bit my tongue.

But I don't mince my words when I write about them or when I speak in public about them.

For instance, I'm outraged by their vendetta against anyone connected with the old Government Accountability Board. And I was disgusted by Fitzgerald and the state senate voting to fire the administrators of the Ethics Commission and Elections Commission just because they both used to work for the GAB, regardless of whether they were deeply involved in the *John Doe II* prosecution or not. And they weren't, by the way. And that prosecution was legitimate because there was ample evidence that Scott Walker was breaking the law on the books at the time that said you can't, as a candidate, coordinate with outside groups that are also engaging in electioneering. The only reason Walker got away with it was because the conservatives on the Wisconsin Supreme Court, who benefited from millions of dollars in expenditures by some of the same outside groups that the *John Doe* prosecutor was going after, waved their magic gavel and said that the First Amendment prohibits the State of Wisconsin from banning coordination between candidates and issue advocacy groups.

To take revenge, Walker and Fitzgerald and Vos have been going after anyone who used to work at the Government Accountability Board. They want to set an example. They want to say, "If you cross us, we're going to crush you!"

And so Fitzgerald and the Republican senators fired Brian Bell at the Ethics Commission and Michael Haas at the Elections Commission without even allowing them a public hearing. This was the first time in the history of Wisconsin that nominees weren't allowed a hearing so they could defend their good names and so the public could weigh in.

To me, this smacked of McCarthyism, and I said so.

To me, Fitzgerald was acting like a playground bully, and I said so.

To me, Fitzgerald was even acting like a wannabe mobster, and I said so. He was trying to rub out anyone who was related to anybody who went after his buddies.

And Dave Zweifel, the great emeritus editor of the *Capital Times*, said so too, writing that Fitzgerald was acting "like a mafia don."

So, the question is, was I being disrespectful to Scott Fitzgerald?

Was Dave Zweifel being disrespectful to Scott Fitzgerald?

I'm going to leave those questions hanging, at least for the moment, because I'd like to throw Trump into the mix too.

Let me level with you: I believe Donald Trump poses an urgent and immediate threat to our democracy. He has attacked the media, the Fourth Estate, as "the enemy of the people," which is something that dictators say. He has attacked the judiciary in ways that we haven't seen in my adult lifetime. He has a fascination with strongmen—not just Putin in Russia but Duterte in the Philippines, and others. And now he wants a military parade!

Let me be blunt: I'm deeply concerned that Trump is a kind of Fascist. He uses two of the calling cards of the Fascist. He traffics in racism, as we saw in the beginning of his campaign, as he railed against Muslims and Mexicans, and as we saw clearly after Charlottesville. And he traffics in ultranationalism. That's what "Make America Great" is all about: it's an appeal to people's sense of aggrieved national pride, and that appeal was central to Mussolini's and Hitler's rise to power.

Racism and ultranationalism are the sperm and the egg of Fascism, and Trump is putting them together with a little *in vitro* fertilization right there in the Oval Office.

And so I use the *F* word—"Fascism"—in public about Trump.

Is that being disrespectful?

And so I call him "Trumpolini."

Is that being disrespectful?

Let's take a couple more examples.

Was it "disrespectful" for the cartoonist David Levine during the Vietnam War to draw his famous cartoon of LBJ? Here's the context: LBJ had just had his appendix removed and liked to show off his scar to everyone, and David Levine made the scar into a map of Vietnam.

Was it "disrespectful" for the cartoonist Herb Block to draw Nixon always having a huge Pinocchio nose and a five o'clock shadow?

Fast forward to the present:

Is it "disrespectful" for Stephen Colbert to make fun of Trump night after night?

Is it "disrespectful" for Alec Baldwin to imitate and parody Trump on *Saturday Night Live*?

Is it "disrespectful" for Colin Kaepernick and other NFL players not to stand for the singing of the national anthem?

I suppose it depends on your definition of "disrespectful."

But here's where I come down:

In a democracy, we actually need to leave room for the disrespectful; we need to respect the disrespectful. We, as Americans, have the right to be disrespectful. We are not living in a monarchy. We do not bow and curtsy to our leaders.

And the demand to be respectful violates the First Amendment and our tradition of free speech and free-wheeling political debate and political satire.

After all, the First Amendment does not say, "Congress shall make no law abridging the freedom of *respectful* speech." It just says, "Congress shall make no law abridging the freedom of speech," with no modifier whatsoever.

And that's how it should be.

So you may conclude that my calling Fitzgerald "a wannabe mobster" was disrespectful, or my calling the man in the White House "Trumpolini" was disrespectful.

If so, so be it.

The imperative to be respectful can turn into a gag order. And I don't like gag orders. They stifle democracy, and we don't want that to happen.

And for me, ultimately, if it's a choice between being "respectful" and telling the truth, I'll tell the truth, with clarity but not vulgarity, colorfully but not crudely. And I won't be rude in person.

That's where I draw the line. You may draw the line somewhere else.

That's something we can debate—respectfully, I hope.

How to Avoid Burnout:
A Guide for Activists

My year-end advice for prodemocracy activists as we turned the corner to 2016.

One thing that concerns me, the older I get, is that we in the peace, justice, and democracy movement need to make sure that we don't burn out and that our colleagues don't burn out and that the generations behind us don't burn out.

We've got to grow our ranks of activists; we can't run them—or ourselves—into the ground.

So here are some "Dos and Don'ts for Activists."

1. Do have fun while you work.
2. Do surround yourself with interesting, smart, fun, kind, and moral people.
3. Do compliment your colleagues and allies on the good work they're doing.
4. Do take vacations.
5. Do set short-term, achievable goals.
6. Do celebrate small victories.
7. Do have healthy hobbies outside of work.
8. Do seek out positive signs and developments.
9. Do remember, you're part of a tremendous historical movement for peace and justice, with inspiring forebearers who faced more daunting challenges than you.
10. Do prepare for the long haul.

—

1. Don't overwork. (Don't work on weekends unless it's an absolute emergency.)
2. Don't become embittered that you're working harder or longer than others.
3. Don't make petty criticisms of coworkers or allies or talk behind their backs.
4. Don't play power games.
5. Don't let your ego get out of control.
6. Don't be a perfectionist.
7. Don't worry about pleasing everyone.
8. Don't generalize about, or demonize, everyone who disagrees with you.
9. Don't keep score.
10. Don't expect immediate success.